Cold Tea and Dust

*Reflections on the complexity of grief,
in prose and poetry*

Susan Elizabeth Elliot

Q

First published in Great Britain in 2023 by Quacks Books
An imprint of Radius Publishing Limited
7 Grape Lane, York, YO1 7HU

Copyright © Susan Elizabeth Elliot

The moral right of Susan Elizabeth Elliot to be identified as
the author of this work has been asserted in accordance
with the Copyright, Designs and Patents Act of 1988.

All rights reserved. No part of this publication may be
reproduced, stored in a retrieval system, or transmitted
in any form or by any means, electronic, mechanical,
photocopying, recording, or otherwise, without the
prior permission of both the copyright owner and the
above publisher of this book.

A CIP catalogue record for this book is
available from the British Library.

isbn 978-1-912728-79-4

Page size 210 x 297 with a gutter margin of 25mm, head 20mm, fore-edge 20mm and foot of 25mm, printed litho on a one hundred gsm bookwove chosen for its sustainability.

Dedicated to the memory of my mother:

Mrs. Doris Mill, (10/12/1913 – 7/6/2003)

'Tell me about despair, yours, and I will tell you mine'.

(Mary Oliver, 'Wild Geese')

Foreword

*Your silver tea set in the hall
catches the sunbeams,*

*and in the absurd aftermath of your dying,
I see you pouring tea –
for you and me.*

In June 2003, my 89 year-old mother paid privately to have a colonoscopy, (a so-called 'routine' procedure), at her age not relishing the prospect of a long wait within the NHS. In the process, the surgeon perforated the bowel, which disaster required emergency abdominal surgery. She then contracted the major infection, Clostridium Difficile, and after a month of suffering and indignity in the care of the health services, both private and public, she died a very miserable, messy death.

My tortuous 'journey' through the grieving that followed was the result of a number of factors: the nature of her death; my spending three years afterwards pursuing an enquiry; our intensely close relationship; my already full bank of loss, including bereavement in childhood.

My decision to complain was prompted firstly by the registrar saying:

'Too many elderly people are dying like this at that hospital. Someone needs to be asking questions.'

My aim was to make positive changes in order to prevent such a tragedy happening to anyone else. It was nothing to do with revenge, which is not always sweet anyway, or financial reward. Later the minister conducting the funeral service likewise commented:

'This was dreadful. Susan needs to be asking questions'.

In the *'appalling aftermath'* as I describe it in the poem, I wrote an account as a kind of therapy. I have revised it here in the context of the aftermath of the Covid 19 pandemic of 2020 - 2022, where at the time of writing, the public enquiry into the government's handling of the crisis is ongoing. So many issues resonate with me. We are grappling with shocking revelations about poor planning and incompetence, power games and an overall 'toxic culture' among those responsible. Bereaved families are already complaining of their lack of a voice alongside the pain of loss. During the crisis, we heard numerous stories of relatives being unable to visit the sick and dying, how in abiding by the rules of conduct, they were forced into communicating artificially, separated by windows or glass screens. Many were unable to say a proper 'goodbye'.

Being *'robbed of the ritual of saying goodbye to loved ones'* means that *the 'link to the past and continuity with familiar objects......are abruptly severed, along with the tie to parts of the self that are left behind as well'.*[1]

At least I was physically present all through my mother's illness, by her bedside when she drew her last breath. I cannot imagine how these families will find 'closure', an elusive concept anyway, especially with anxiety about the state of our health service remaining at an all-time high, so that the subject is never far from our minds. Then last winter we heard other stories of patients dying in parked ambulances or hospital corridors, people losing their lives through lack of adequate resources and competent management.

We've since seen a plethora of studies in academic circles[2] considering the nature of so-called 'complicated grief', in order to organise treatment. It has a number of other labels: 'prolonged grief', 'traumatic grief' or 'persistent complex grief' and has been added to the DSM -5[3] as a mental disorder. A set of symptoms has been identified:

'a preoccupation with grief and feelings of loss to the point of clinically significant distress and impairment, leading to depression, emotional pain, numbness, loneliness, identity disturbance and difficulty in managing interpersonal relationships, plus a sense of meaninglessness.'

According to the research, 10% of 'survivors' suffer in this way.

No one in our country has challenged the need for an investigation, but such was not always my experience. I had to manage my frustration and hurt when even close friends expressed intolerance. I became exhausted eventually with the sheer amount of paper work that the complaints involved, including numerous exchanges of letters and reports. It became obvious that I had to pay meticulous attention to detail throughout, as some people were intent at tripping me up. Writing poems then gave huge emotional and spiritual release, leading me on to study the link between loss and poetry and using the subject as the focus of my dissertation when later embarking on a degree in Creative Writing.

One of the main issues in relation to my mother's care was the fragmentation of services, alongside numerous other factors leading to stress and burnout amongst individual staff members. To my mind, the split between the public and private sector was clearly one of these. 20 years later little appears to have changed. The pandemic has in fact highlighted long-term organisational problems and huge discontent in the ranks. Already this year Britain has been

---

[1] *Hollander, N.C. 1998.*
[2] *The Centre for Prolonged Grief, Columbia University School of Social Work*
[3] *Diagnostic and Statistical Manual of Mental Illnesses – the latest edition of the American Psychiatric Association's professional reference book on mental health and brain-related conditions.*

torn apart with strikes. For the first time in the history of the NHS, nurses, junior doctors, ambulance drivers and even consultants have been on picket lines fighting for the pay and the fair conditions they richly deserve. I was in awe of their dedication and bravery through the pandemic, and remain so, even though my mother's experience had been so negative.

Revising any piece of writing can bring major shifts in perspective, and such has certainly been true for me. My mother of course has no voice with which to tell her own story, or to respond to my analysis of our relationship. The determination and energy that kept me fighting for answers about her death, and in many other challenging situations in my life, has though come from her example.

Particular thanks are due to my friend and fellow writer, Jacqueline Everett, who provided valuable suggestions on structure and gave such positive encouragement. Also thanks to my husband James for proofreading, not to mention his endless patience and understanding. He too supported my conviction that my mother's story needed to be told. It has taken me all this time to assemble the various components and the reader will find an array of writing styles from straightforward narrative to formal reports, academic analysis, poetry, and my attempts at prose poems. I hope though the work 'hangs together' and is not too arduous to follow. Above all, I hope it will be of use.

The identities of the organisations involved have been anonymised.

October 2023

My Floury Mother – A Life

Growing up in Wales

My mother, being the youngest of seven children, was born in an old thatched cottage in the little hamlet of South Cornelly, in between Cardiff and Swansea near the South Wales coast. She spent her childhood in the seaside town of Porthcawl, where the family's finances became so stretched in The Depression that they took in visitors to make ends meet: Mum described a house alive with people, thriving on the company and the fun. She developed talents in all practical skills, winning a prize for pastry-making at the age of 14. Her ambition was to be a children's nurse, but as her sister Gwen was already in nurse training and Victoria pursuing a career as a music teacher, there was no money left to support her professionally. Tradition too was that the youngest daughter was designated to work in the home and be available to care for elderly parents.

Mum on the left, second row, next to her father

So she stayed put and worked as a dressmaker, subsequently also covering suites of furniture for a few pounds. This enabled her to take singing lessons with the Professor of Music at Cardiff University. She joined the local Operatic Society, taking many leading roles over the years, including that of 'Magnolia' in 'Showboat'. Her fellow performers there called her *'The Mighty Atom'*; although just five foot, she was a formidable young woman with a magnetic personality.

In 1938 her father had a stroke and she gave up sewing to look after him until he died after which she became ill with nervous exhaustion. During the war she was a postwoman, making as many as three deliveries a day, mainly to a number of army camps based in the town. Towards the end of the conflict she worked for the Refuge Assurance Company, disliking the sales part of the job, but loving to meet new people with their warm Welsh welcome.

Marriage – the move to London

Through a mutual friend, Mum had been writing to an English soldier, Archie Mill, who was serving in the Royal Artillery, undertaking dangerous missions and without a girlfriend to link with for support. Determined to escape the confines of home, she married him in 1948, initially living in a tiny terraced house with my paternal grandparents in New Malden. Encouraged by my kind father, she was accepted into the Royal Choral Society, singing in the Royal Albert Hall under the direction of Sir Malcolm Sargent, whilst receiving individual tuition at the Royal Academy of Music. This was funded by my father, who as a railway clerk in Camden Town earned £7-10s a week. The lessons each cost £1-10s.

At the Academy my mother was encouraged to pursue a solo career, but I came along in 1949. We moved to a neglected Victorian house in Balham a year later. Mum described a premises with bomb-damaged walls, damp, and with cockroaches crawling in the basement. My parents worked hard together to restore this their first home, even turning their hands to bricklaying, exterminating the unwanted insect life, decorating rooms (another of Mum's many skills), and planting the garden. There were holidays too with the family back in Wales.

My grandparents, Mum, friend Gillian (right) and me (left). My Dad might have taken this early photo. We all look so happy.

~

I was just three years old during Christmas 1952 when the Great Smog hit the city. My father made paper lanterns to drape all over the banisters and up the stairs, little silver bells made of cigarette paper and tin foil to hang on the tree. The smog had been one of the worst London had endured and must have affected him, commuting to his boring job. His main ambition, being highly intelligent and with a passion for reading, was to own a bookshop. He had served all the way through the war in a number of countries, on several occasions narrowly escaping fatal explosions.

During another foggy night in March 1953, my 36 year-old father suddenly turned over in bed and died from a massive coronary.

So I'm to die now, like this, not in the heat of battle with guns blazing,
but in a bed in Balham, my little wife gently snoring.

I'm not one for talking; prefer reading, anything I can get.
Now that's all finished. I'm a shy man, given

to quiet introspection, thoughts of peace. 'You're too kind', she said.
I had to join up, with a father scarred by the trench.

I've never told her the full story: how sleeping with dead animals
made me vomit. How I longed for suburbia and apple blossom.

It's been a strange life, growing up in the shadow of war; a silent father,
puzzled mother, our small lives.

I did my best out there, observing, then a job that's brought
money but boredom,

travelling in crowded trains with pale office boys, dreaming lost dreams
in smoky tunnels. We found a place

we could call our own, cheap and rotten from bombs. Worked like crazy
to build up, repair. Took in lodgers,

built walls, dug the garden. We were ready to plant. Last Christmas
I made paper lanterns,

hung them over banisters and stairs, bright paper chains from light fittings.
But now in the smog of March

a blood clot is winding its rogue way through the terrace of veins.
I won't see day, watch my child grow.

Remember me and my unlived life.

Mum was left with a small widow's pension so had to go out to work. I can remember her wheeling me in my pushchair to a plastic lampshade factory on Tooting Bec Common behind our house, where she stayed for a while until the acrid fumes began to affect her beautiful soprano voice. I have no memories of my father, but have his books, and every Christmas I put the little silver bells, which have miraculously survived, on our tree.

I have often wondered about this photo – my mother looks strained and my grandparents so concerned about her. Where is it? Who took it? Why?

~

Going Home

Towards the late 1950's, seeing my mother struggling on in the city, Mum's brother suggested she return to Porthcawl to help in his grocery shop. Although she felt wary about giving up her own home and looking after older relatives again, she felt there was little choice. One Sunday morning she felt so depressed she missed the customary church service and spent the time instead cooking all my father's favourite cakes, so many that the family couldn't eat them all. Her brother Rees took the remainder to the shop to sell and the following day his customers returned to ask for more. The rest is history.

After this first success, despite much discouragement, if not opposition from the bank manager: *'You'll never make a go of it! Stay at home and look after your child!'* Mum bought a premises opposite the grocery and opened a bakery: *'Elizabeth's Home-Made Cakes'*, so named after her mother who had taught her to cook. Its popularity grew over the years, and she opened a little teashop too in the back room. In addition to the staff, as a family we all helped out during busy periods such as Christmas, which for me was the highlight of the year.

Christmas Eve at Elizabeth's - 1961

(with apologies to Dylan Thomas)

In the sticky-out town poking its nose in the rumpled channel,
daring to stare at the English, the streets are hushed,
steam from the last trains long since dry on windows.

Billy the Beat is satisfied that all is well. Thomas the Fish
can take a welcome rest: we'll all be having turkey,
ham, pork, chicken, sides of beef cut from the hills.

The lights are on in Morgan the Meat, whose wig is already askew.
He chops and slices, watches the blood ooze on the sawdust,
wipes his red nose on his spotted apron.

Davies the Milk counts his bottles, Williams the Death
checks the bodies for signs of resurrection:
sniffs the sour air in satisfaction.

Our house stirs. It is 3 o'clock; no hint of the sun
which will lift itself from the sea when it's ready.

My mother leads the way on her wartime bike.
I ride whilst she pushes, loving the feel
of the tyres over drains and ruts.

*The family will follow after breakfast:
bacon, egg, laverbread, sarm.* [4]

*She's iced two hundred Christmas cakes,
will make five times that in mince pies,
three hundred puddings, dozens of welsh-cakes,
teisan lap*[5], *pasties for the men boozing in 'the Social',
sausage rolls, chocolate logs, custard slices,
butterfly buns sprinkled with stardust for the children.*

*We pass over the railway: the sensation of rubber
on rusting steel. Parry the Paper lifts his bales
from the frosty pavement and retreats into dark.*

The sharp air is windless.

*Usually this flatulent coast boasts wild seas,
holds rock pools in permanent shimmer,
boats in the broth of the harbour disco dance and jive
to the croak of grey gulls, waves scud the mud,
slap the old walls pock-marked with soot.*

*It's not a posh shop, but spotless. A bell clangs
to warn of custom – not that anyone's dishonest.
We feed the few tramps for free with more than just leftovers.*

*The kettle goes on, we laugh, something I love to see
in my sad parent who's come alive with the flour and sugar,
butter, eggs. Even onions don't make her cry:
she's immune to pain after the heat of pans
and baking trays has burnt rings on flesh.*

*Meantime hair has turned to white wire,
there are dashes on cheeks sallow from summer,
where spattered batter finds her deep early lines.
At last the tribe arrives: uncles and aunts don overalls.*

'Showed up, have you?!'

*I'm only small but my tasks are as crucial:
heaped teaspoons of mincemeat in pastry shells –*

'Not too much, mind, or too little.'

---

[4] *laverbread is a seaweed, delicious when fried; sarm is the Welsh for fried bread*
[5] *a kind of fruit loaf – pronounced 'teeshun'*

I spread the chocolate on the logs.

'Don't forget to dig in the Santas!'

*Soon the poetry of finding fun in work reverberates
to the clatter of Kenwoods, the hum of ovens.
The sun joins in, scars the hilltops, casts orange
on black rock, gold on sand where curlews and dunlins pace the shore.*

*By late afternoon there's little left, the brown lino is encrusted
with crumbs that stick to heels. We sit and gossip in the thick air;
how it looks as if Beryl's been at the gin:*

'What a state to be in!

*How Haelwen's voice
is like a whistle through sea grass:*

'We'll soon be needing hearing aids!'

*How Annie Eynon's skirts
barely cover her knickers:
'But did you see that bruise?!'*

*'Castrate the bugger, I would.
Cut it off with my pair of pinking scissors!'*

*By evening, the place gleams with bleach,
even the back yard scrubbed
on hands and knees.*

*My mother switches off the lights.
As we leave her mouth droops.*

*I dream of Barry the Bank,
who bought the last mince pies
and told us to go easy on the sherry.*

~

Mum's day usually started at about 4 a.m. ending in the early evening, often longer hours in peak periods. She was so successful that she paid off the bank loan within the decade; the new bank manager was astounded at her perseverance. The price she paid for all the hard work in later life was persistent pain in her legs. She retired in 1973, occupying herself with church activities, singing semi-professionally, and inevitably, supporting her ageing siblings.

Mum outside the shop, 1969

My Floury Mother

So where are you now, my floury mother?
In what welsh cake heaven are you
sifting sugar, cracking eggs?
Are you floating on coconut clouds, or
treading on marzipan, swimming in savoury seas,
in waves of puff pastry, or basking in basins of batter?
Are you skating on almond slice ice,
walking in hazelnut hills, or snoozing on syrup?
Do your eyes glisten with onion peel tears,
are there yellow scones for tea,
with cheese from Caerphilly? Dewberry jam?
Do you watch your yeast cakes
rising in the East? Is your lap full of teisan?

Come, shake out your wire tray hair,
hang up your white apron, engulf me in dust,
a confectionery kiss, before we
fall asleep on a chocolate log,
or an apple pie bed
in cream custardy sheets
dreaming of vanilla sponge love.

By 1998 Mum and Auntie Gwen were the only two family members left alive. After much deliberation, they decided to move to a sheltered accommodation complex on the south coast, (Malvern Court), where a team of staff was on site 24 hours daily. Workmen were available to carry out repairs and do odd jobs and a restaurant and regular social events completed the package. Amenities within a stone's throw included a supermarket and a health centre. There was no such facility in York. My cousin Margaret and her husband Cyril, to whom they were close, were retired and living locally, whereas James and I were still in employment. We continued to visit regularly, and they often came to stay with us.

I will remember my mother as a woman of many colours: sensitive, warm, loving and fun-loving, generous, strong, determined and passionate, never lukewarm about anything. Loyal in all her relationships, she was also sensitive to hurt, but although craving connection to others, she could be quite relaxed in her own company. In addition to being a wonderful cook, she was a born manager, like her mother before her. Deeply religious, her faith always sustained her.

Mum sacrificed everything for me: taught me to read before starting school so that I had a head start educationally, supported me through university and beyond into my career, respecting my decision to enter social work, taking great pride in all my achievements, and suffering with me in my setbacks.

I vividly remember one night during the anxious time when I was taking my 'A' levels, a period when she pulled out all the stops to support me:

Storm

Three weeks, sleepless, in a vacuum with Brahms and Shakespeare,
Baudelaire and Bach; the mind stored facts, quotes, themes, ready for test.
You and I had walked from house to shore.

It was either very late or early; the sea mist must have got into memory.
Along the promenade we watched the lightening forks pierce the horizon,
punch the flat sea. The rock pools shimmered, like my cheap coat.

Pebbles shifted, porcelain houses gleamed in unearthly light.
The planet, on a brink of dissolution, shuddered in thunder.
Our eyes followed the path of the storm. We stood there a lifetime,

traced the migraine tracks from west to east and back again,
around promontories, ancient stone. You gripped my hand,
the other on rail. I saw your white knuckles on iron, felt muscles clench.

We wondered if it would reach us, obliterate our small town, or move on.
But somehow what happened then is lost: whether we got drenched in rain,
each other's tears. Then the air cleared: enough to breathe and sleep again.

In the process of writing the poem, which started out as a simple memory, I later came to see that the electricity pulsing through the elements was symbolic. Alongside my mother's clenched muscles and 'white knuckles', not only did the storm stress our heightened mental state, but maybe there was also an unspoken awareness that passing the exams and going to university would mean a first separation from each other. I shall explore other poems in a later section.

As mother and daughter, both of whose lives had been profoundly affected by our shared bereavement, we were thrown together into an intense relationship. At the same time, whilst Mum could talk openly of her loss, the impact on me was never discussed. Growing up (and into adulthood), I often felt rendered powerless by her despair, and as I struggled to find my own way in life, there were the inevitable conflicts. I explore these later, a process which has proved as challenging without her presence as it had been when she was alive.

'No relationship is as highly charged as that between mother and daughter, or as riddled with expectations that could, like a landmine, detonate with a single misstep, a solitary stray word that, without warning, wounds or enrages. And no relationship is as bursting with possibilities of goodwill and understanding.' (Secunda, V. in Exley, H. 1995)

With Mum and Auntie Gwen in York

A Death Not Worth Dying For

'It's that much heralded thing, the quality of life that is important. How you live your life, what you get out of it, what you put into it and what you leave behind after it. We should aim for a good and rich life well lived, and at the end of it, in the comfort of our own home, in the company of those who love us, have a death worth dying for.'

(Terry Pratchett, 'Shaking Hands with Death': the BBC Richard Dimbleby Lecture, 2010)

Some time ago I read a profile of Julia Margaret Cameron, the Victorian photographer. She had a full and successful life, surrounded by friends and family, inspired by beauty, captured so well on camera. The manner of her dying whilst living in her son's house in Ceylon was by all accounts, rather special. Suddenly sitting up in bed to watch the stars she exclaimed: *'Beautiful!'* before sinking back into the sheets.

I was left wondering how it is that some are blessed with a peaceful end, or even with such an experience of joy like this, and why for others it is ghastly. A friend of mine who lost her husband a couple of months after my mother died, described his death as *'good'*. He had enjoyed a long and happy marriage with four children and many grandchildren. After a series of minor strokes he lost consciousness before *'passing peacefully away'* in the presence of his family in his own home.

Another memory is of my mother describing the death of a family friend; someone she had known since childhood, and for whom she always had ambivalent feelings. 'Auntie M' had died very peacefully in her sleep. *'Trust her!'* my mother had seethed, (rather unkindly I thought at the time), as if she anticipated the opposite. Three or four months before she met her untimely end, she described a terrible nightmare where she was wading through acres of mud. I felt the chill of premonition.

~

Auntie Gwen died in 2001 after a series of strokes and after much deliberation Mum stayed on in their flat. Despite problems with arthritis and other maladies, she was determined to keep active and cheerful, but since a hysterectomy in her 70's, she had suffered with what she called her 'lazy bowel'. The condition had become progressively worse during the winter of 2002/3 where persistent diarrhoea prevented her from enjoying her social life. On the recommendation of a friend she saw a consultant surgeon who offered to carry out the colonoscopy in a small private hospital ('The Haven') adjacent to the general hospital in the same town on the south coast. As a family we had never used private health care before and held the NHS in high regard: three members of the family had in fact had careers in nursing.

My mother paid £1386 for the investigation. During the course of a brief telephone discussion I had with the consultant to discuss risk, he informed me that the only problem he foresaw was the possible side-effect of the anaesthetic on someone of Mum's age, although he felt confident, being 'astounded' by the strength of her heart and lungs (maybe thanks to all the singing). As described, he was forced to carry out emergency abdominal surgery, cutting away part of the colon. When Mum was coming round from the anaesthetic, in pain, distress and confusion, I witnessed the anaesthetist leaning over her:

'Mrs. Mill….you did sign the consent form, didn't you?'

My mother remained in great discomfort for a week, on various drips, and suffering with a urine infection. She then began to suffer copious diarrhoea. Still in shock myself, I imagined at first that this was as a result of the surgery which had doubtless weakened her damaged bowel. At the same time I had been relieved to know that there was 'no cancer'. When problem showed no sign of abating, seeing my mother so sick and exhausted, I began to wonder what was really going on.

There was one ward sister who never acknowledged me as I arrived to visit, always looking down at her paper work as I approached. She was on duty the day I decided to press for an answer. Saying nothing, with pursed lips she marched into my mother's room and literally slammed a leaflet down on the bedside table, before walking back to the privacy of her desk. This described a new infection that I had never heard of. It was aptly named, a very difficult infection indeed.

The incontinence went on for another ten days, during which time Mum was treated with antibiotics. Although nursing and medical care was on the whole good, I had the uneasy feeling that she was being pressurised to 'get better'. The surgeon also quietly told me that the anaesthetist had 'waived his fee'. I wondered why, but hesitated to ask more questions, fearing reprisals in the quality of care. We were both in their hands.

The kitchen staff failed to acknowledge Mum's dietary needs as an elderly woman with a serious bowel condition, and feeling sick all the time. Despite my protestations they continued to send up rich three-course meals, the sight and smell of which made her retch, and none of which she could eat. After three weeks she had lost much weight, was unable to dress, wash and toilet herself and only able to take short walks down the ward corridor with the aid of a frame and staff member for support. I discovered that discharge plans were being discussed in the early morning ward round before I had arrived for the day.

With great difficulty I managed to get a hearing with the consultant, who confessed that he was being *'leant upon by the administration'*. He reported my mother as having responded to antibiotics and free of the bouts of diarrhoea, if only for two or three days. He didn't want to transfer her to an NHS ward where he feared she would get depressed, if not institutionalised. I could understand this, whilst sensing an underlying agenda which filled me with trepidation. Then suddenly he made the bizarre suggestion that I take her out for a cream tea: my desperately weak mother, trying to recover from a major assault on her small body and still hardly able to stand.

Struggling with a chaos of feelings, I thought that perhaps he was stressed himself, perhaps anxious about his own competence and maybe fearing reprisals. On the other hand, he had all the power. Had it not been for the fact that Mum was agitating for discharge herself, together with my fears that she might catch yet another infection if she stayed in hospital, I would have fought this decision tooth and nail.

Four days before Mum was discharged, she fainted twice and fell on the toilet floor. I was told this was *'normal in the circumstances'*. Two days later she refused to get up. I tearfully begged her to try to summon up some energy. On the day before discharge she had obviously made a massive effort to be positive and asked me to bring her some clothes to wear on the journey home. Much later during the enquiry I saw a letter from the consultant to Mum's GP, which described her as *'amazingly active and agile.'* This was unbelievable nonsense.

Within hours of discharge she relapsed, with a return of the vicious infection, leaving her doubly incontinent again. The mess and the stench pervaded the normally spotless flat. I was glad Auntie Gwen wasn't there. During the early hours I phoned the night staff of the Haven to be told that Mum could only be readmitted via her GP. I later found out that under the terms of the contract, she had immediate readmission rights in the event of relapse following surgery. Of this the ward sister was patently unaware, as was I.

I subsequently phoned the on-call GP, (working in a contracted-out service), who refused to make a home visit and told me *'not to give her any dairy produce.'*

During the course of the following morning my mother was soiling herself continuously; it was taking four of us to clean her up. The staff at the housing complex helping me were concerned about the risk of infection to the other residents, being all too aware that they were soon due to serve lunch. At 8.30 a.m. I phoned the local practice, explaining the urgency of the situation, to be told that Mum's GP could only visit after morning surgery. She finally turned up at 1 p.m., took one brief look, heard about the events of the previous three weeks (of which she was unaware despite my report to the receptionist), and arranged for an urgent admission to the local general hospital. Mum was by now refusing to go back to the Haven anyway.

At the general hospital my mother was moved between three different wards over the next six days. The first – an isolation room on the admission ward – hadn't been cleaned for the previous 48 hours due to staff sickness, plus absence due to training. There was no hot running water available and restorations to the ward above meant that drilling was going on all day.

On admission, the ward staff made no attempt whatsoever to talk to me. They persistently refused to hear my account of what had taken place over the previous three weeks, saying they would carry out their own assessment. My mother by now was severely dehydrated. I went in search of water and had to wait several minutes at the nursing station, listening to the nurses talking amongst themselves about the latest episode of 'Coronation Street', before they supplied me with the same. Returning to the isolation room, I found my mother distressed. An auxiliary nurse was occupied with trying to clean her up, shouting at her to *'lift your bottom!'*

Mum implored me not to *'let that nurse touch me again!'* so I told her to leave, and soon afterwards the ward sister came marching in, accusing me of *'upsetting her staff'*. At that point I became emotional myself, pointing out how very stressful the previous few weeks had been for all of us, most of all, my mother. Later two nurses turned up to try unsuccessfully to administer a saline drip. One of them joked to me that she was *'still learning'*.

On the second day Mum was transferred to a rehabilitation ward for head-injured patients. Two members of staff confided that they were feeling too unwell themselves to be on duty, and the (kindly and clearly stressed) ward sister admitted to shortages, especially on the night shift. Mum continued to be unwell, spending tracts of time shivering on the toilet wrapped in a blanket, one of numerous pathetic images which stay with me. Moreover, she complained of rough treatment by the night staff, begging me to take her away. But I had nowhere safe to take her. I felt utterly powerless.

At the weekend and seemingly without supervision, two junior doctors had still failed to sort out the drip. It had leaked during the night and the bedclothes were saturated when I visited at 2 p.m. the following afternoon. Staff were generally uncommunicative, and did not appear to know about previous events. One nurse asked me to complete a form making plans for Mum's discharge. This was two days before she was to die.

I found myself responding to questions about her hobbies and interests in a daze. When asked to describe the facilities at Malvern Court, this nurse retorted: *'It's all right for some!'* No precautions were made against the risk of thrombosis, such as compression stockings, despite my protestations. Senior medical staff were notably absent and I felt that junior medics were unconfident and missing crucial symptoms: my mother appeared to be vomiting blood.

By now acutely sensitive to what was happening around us, I picked up a substantial level of (understandable) resentment about staff in the NHS having to remedy faults made in the private sector. In other words, value judgements were clearly being made.

On Sunday June 8th during my customary morning phone call to the ward, I was informed that Mum had had a *'more settled'* night. I went for a walk, the first in ages, taking my mobile and leaving the answer phone on in the flat. I received no messages on either. When I arrived on the ward at about 1 p.m. there was no sign of Mum. The agency nurse had no idea where she had gone as she hadn't had time to read the notes.

After a few phone calls it was discovered she had been taken to the ward for the elderly, the very one that the consultant had dreaded admitting her the week before. On arrival I was greeted, this time sympathetically, by a nurse who told me gently that Mum was now *'very ill indeed'*. She was hyperventilating, on oxygen, and the registrar on duty had been trying to get a feeder tube into her neck for some time, as by now her once beautiful hands were swollen like balloons from all the botched attempts at administering a drip. That evening Mum begged me not to leave her, but the nurses were concerned not only that I should get some rest, but that they could continue with their attempts to save her.

I felt so torn, wanting to stay by her bedside, distressing as it was to see her, but realised it was better for me to give the staff some space. I stayed in the day room down the corridor all night with my cousin, trying in vain to catch some sleep on the hard plastic chairs, but instead watching the nurses and doctors come and go, hoping against hope for any signs of progress. Their care and sensitivity was in stark contrast to what had gone before, but sadly too late. At 4 a.m. the registrar broke the news that she had done all she could and the prognosis was grave. She was clearly upset. By her own admission she was *'astounded'* by what she had now learned of Mum's prior ordeal.

At 9 a.m. next day, not having slept a wink, I attended the ward meeting. The discussion was stiff and formal; I tried to listen to the consultant's medical terminology and assessment of my mother's present condition. I said little, being exhausted and quietly furious, but remember saying:

'You all need to know how angry I am'.

The junior doctor who had persistently failed to insert a drip over previous days, looked down at the floor. Being acutely aware of the group dynamics, I had the distinct impression that a young male doctor was stifling suppressed laughter. I remembered how a couple of years previously I had read a newspaper article: an account by a grieving mother describing a similar occurrence when attending the inquest after her young son's death, where she was aware of *'sniggering and giggling'*. Anxiety does strange things.

All that morning I stayed with Mum, attending to the simple tasks to which I was by now accustomed: moistening her cracked lips, cooling her hot forehead, all the while watching the struggle for breath, seeing the ghastly yellow bruising on her neck and chest. I held her swollen hands, leaving only when the nurses had to come and clean her up, as the bouts of diarrhoea continued right up until the moment of death. She remained mentally alert, which was amazing given her terrible state, yet additionally cruel in its own way.

'Sue love, don't make a fuss'.

I knew of course what these simple words meant: a mother's instinct to protect, knowing what a strain on me it would be. I gave a non-committal reply, whilst realising how aware she always was of how strongly I felt about any injustice. And I hope now, how much I loved her.

Towards 1 p.m. she turned towards me, pleading for the nurses to *'take out all these wires'*. She had had enough. I left the room, at which point she started shouting one last time that the diarrhoea was *'coming again!'* Two nurses rushed in, calling to me a few minutes later:

'Come quickly, she's fading fast!'

There were no parting words of endearment; she was simply absenting herself. Momentarily I hated her for seeming to leave me in such a dispassionate way, this mother who had been so warm and affectionate. During the last moments I had the uncanny impression of something being sucked out of her and found myself hoping it was her spirit ascending. Then it dawned on me that it was 'just' her lungs collapsing. A pulmonary embolism had finally killed her.

This wasn't the parting I had imagined for us, I needed something positive to hold on to, even a simple smile, like the one my aunt had given me after her strokes, and which comforts me still. This death was the complete opposite: cold and hateful, leaving a gaping chasm of grief, filling up rapidly with a thousand questions.

Minutes later, we were ushered forcibly out of the room. The young doctor rushed in to check that Mum had indeed 'gone', before running to another room where I heard her making a phone call. I was completely ignored, later realising this was to arrange a post mortem as the consultant had picked up my possible intention to complain.

The ward sister had in the meantime come on duty. She ushered us into her office and gave us cups of tea. I couldn't cry, being numb from anger and exhaustion, so instead put on my social work hat and had a discussion about the current state of the NHS. She pointed to her desk which was piled high with paper work.

'See all this?' she said. *'I refuse to play this game, they'll just have to wait for all their forms and reports. I need to be on the ward to supervise the real work.'*

In the evening the shock propelled me into an awful state of agitation, alone in Mum's flat. After a very large gin, I made a load of phone calls, first to James of course, then even to friends I did not consider close. Into the sleepless night I made a start on preparing a letter of complaint to the NHS Trust, having been given an information leaflet from the ward sister. It was months before I could shed a tear, the various emotional states in this first 'stage' of grief feeling like a hurricane in my brain, which otherwise remained crystal clear about the preceding events.

Even now, 20 years on, it feels like the proverbial yesterday.

~

Sunflower

I wrenched you away, frowned at the earth,
where before you had nodded at the sun
as the day cooled. I felt the thick stem empty,
so broke you in bits. You resisted,

left a breast-shaped dent, a few mangled roots.
I salvaged one or two blooms, dried black seeds
to scatter for the Spring. The lifeless leaves
drooped like the empty sleeves of unused puppets,
the large hearts turned to dust, whilst the roses,
still lingering, mocked your short span of life.
They, after all, had outlasted summer, self-satisfied.

The Enquiry

Between June10th 2003 to July 2006 I was involved with three separate complaints: against The Haven private hospital, the Primary Care Trust, and the NHS hospital. This constituted what one of my university colleagues described as a mammoth project. In addition, as an only child, I had full responsibility for sorting out all the other tasks that follow a bereavement, whilst trying to maintain my demanding career in social work education.

When James and I first came to York in 1990, I took on a post where I was responsible for developing a social work service within an independent psychiatric hospital. I had naively anticipated that I would be made completely welcome. Although in time I developed good working relationships with certain members of staff, especially one of the consultant psychiatrists and the sister in charge of the acute admission ward, trying to establish professional roots was often an uphill battle. This involved challenging various practices which in line with social work values felt questionable, and I was intimidated if not bullied by some individuals. My line manager once called me 'a little terrier'; someone who found it hard to compromise where I felt concerned about standards. Although these wounds may have projected themselves into the situation I now faced, at least the experience had taught me a few valuable lessons.

I approached my enquiry though with a certain measure of guilt. I realised that the pursuit of truth and positive change would cost the services financially, and in terms of time: the need for example to arrange meetings and complete reports and correspondence, taking staff away from direct patient care. As well as the registrar and the Methodist minister, a number of people though were also fully supportive of my actions: my cousin and her husband, who had been consistently appalled by events, as had my own husband James, plus the staff in Malvern Court. The latter were particularly angry about the premature discharge from The Haven, and the refusal of the on-call GP to make a home visit. One person commented that GPs from the local practice were *always reluctant to come out*.

At the time I had little knowledge of the complaints system, the complexity of which seems deliberately designed to put people off. Thankfully my work experience, especially in the role of advocate, also stood me in good stead.

I have tried in the following account to cut down as best I could on the tedious amount of detail, whilst trying to give a picture of what it is like to handle an enquiry on top of coming to terms with major loss. Losing a parent is massive.

~

The Haven

My main concerns about the private hospital were in connection with the consent to treatment procedure; the failure to give appropriate information on risk; the decision-making process towards discharge, with what I perceived to be its political 'agenda'; communication between myself and the staff; the lack of information and staff training on patient rights to re-admission following relapse. For a few months I handled the complaint on my own.

- Consent to treatment

Following consultation with the surgeon, the Director of Nursing wrote to me on his behalf. The former remained adamant that my mother had discussed the procedure fully before admission, that she had signed the consent form then and been told that the main risk *'at any age is bleeding, not perforation.'* I had contacted the NHS Direct help line soon after the first crisis, and was told that the main risk to the elderly in relation to a colonoscopy was definitely perforation. The person I spoke to expressed nothing short of horror at my description of events, suggesting that I should sue the hospital.

- Discharge plans

The consultant asserted that *'he had regular discussions with relatives and always responded to their requests.'* He went on to accuse me of making *'no effort to put anything in place for Mrs. Mill's discharge.'* Both of these statements were complete lies. In reality I had only two face-to-face discussions with him, the first being immediately after the initial crisis, where in fact I had (respectfully) accepted his apology and his explanation for the perforation: that the inflammation in, and associated fragility of, my mother's colon, was much worse than he had anticipated.

The second was the brief appointment in between his clinics at the general hospital. Otherwise as described he did his rounds at The Haven in the early morning before going on duty. I was incensed by his accusation, having had had numerous discussions about discharge plans with the ward sister, none of which had been documented. She had in turn reported problems in communication between the hospital and community services: none had in fact been organised.

I wrote back promptly, defending my position. An apologetic reply came from the Executive Director of the company:

'It is always a difficult situation when one person is trying to respond on behalf of another, especially when medical information is involved.'

Is it?

- Rights to re-admission

I had never seen the documentation given to my mother about the 'package' she had purchased, covering the question of 'complications'. Too late I realised I should have checked this before, but I don't think that I even knew of its existence. Knowing how desperate my mother was I suspected she had never even read it at the time.

When I was finally given access, I discovered that it clearly stated:

'The package covers the cost of any related conditions or complications that become apparent within 30 days of discharge from the hospital following the procedure, provided such conditions or complications are treated at the hospital, and that you have followed the advice of your consultant and other medical professional involved in your treatment. Any related medical condition that arises during your stay will be managed until you are fit for discharge from an acute hospital, at no extra cost.'

Always check the paper work.

I was told that the nurses were to receive a letter informing them of the policy regarding emergency admissions, clearly an omission during preliminary training. Interestingly enough the ward sister was now commenting that *'she was very pleased with the help and support'* she had received from me.

A subsequent report from the consultant hinted at internal struggles within the organisation. He expressed concern for example, at the way in which the letter from the Director of Nursing had been worded. The argument about risk issues continued; he maintained that he had discussed these fully but agreed that I should have been more clearly informed in general. He also confessed that he had been under the impression that his staff had arranged community care. Although he had in fact intimated as such, the report completely denied any *'financial agenda'*. He maintained the strange belief that my mother was *'amazingly fit and active'* prior to discharge, but concurred that I should have been invited to be present to support Mum when the consent form had been produced for signature.

~

I was by now so concerned about the process of this complaint that I contacted the Independent Health Care Association and the National Care Standards Commission, the latter taking up my case two months after my mother had died. The report was ready by October. With regard to informed consent, it emerged that Mum had signed the form just prior to surgery, when she was alone, without support, and on her way to theatre.

'It would appear that the consent form was signed just prior to surgery, not as described ……The anaesthetist, from the records, obtained consent. This is not in accordance with the policy of the hospital and may fall short of the recommendations of the Department of Health and General Medical Council guidance…'

Also *'the information made available to patients in the patient areas regarding colonoscopy does not discuss risks….I was unable to evidence that your mother received this information….without this….it is difficult to evidence informed consent.'* Also there was no evidence that I *'had been given advice about rights of readmission in the event of relapse.'*

It was discovered that the form was primitive in comparison with the one later recommended by the Department of Health as a result of the work of the Consent Advisory Group of July 2003, a first sign perhaps of the clash of culture between private and public health care.

Had I been better informed myself I might have thought twice about encouraging Mum to have the procedure, or at least had the chance to talk it over in greater depth. I had been entirely misled, lulled into inaction by the term 'routine' and the consultant's apparent confidence.

The inspector made several recommendations to address these issues. The Commission was already inspecting the hospital on a yearly basis, and having unearthed numerous problems already, sent me two inspection reports for 2003 and 2004, each over 70 pages long. Reading through the contents I was amazed that the place had been allowed to keep open.

Mum celebrating Christmas with me in my first London flat, 1982

The Primary Care Trust

The second complaint was aimed at the Primary Care Trust responsible for the contracted out GP on-call service. Shortly after I had lodged my concerns, one wet Friday afternoon (that's how vivid the memories are), I had a surprise phone call from my mother's own GP. This was an attempt to persuade me to withdraw, and convince me (unsuccessfully) that the on-call GP in question had managed the situation appropriately. Our hour-long discussion only served to inflame me further. Then, even more dissatisfied with the subsequent protracted internal enquiry, I took the complaint to the next stage: a request for an independent panel hearing.

There was an exchange of letters between the Complaints and Project Manager of the PCT, the Director of the on-call service, the duty doctor I had rung the night Mum relapsed, and the Head of Corporate Affairs at the PCT. This process lasted until October 2003, with a panel hearing eventually taking place in February 2004 over three days. It was held at an exclusive 5* hotel with seven panel members, at least four of whom would have required overnight accommodation there, no doubt costing the NHS a substantial amount. I didn't receive a penny in travel expenses.

I made contact with the local ICAS (Independent Complaints Advocacy Service), a new project managed at that time by the Citizens Advice Bureau. It emerged (via their investigation) that the tape of my conversation with the doctor had been destroyed. The panel concluded that he was culpable in not agreeing to carry out a home visit, especially having discovered through his work log that

'he was under no workload constraint that would have inhibited such a decision.'

They emphasised that he should have taken account of Mum's

'advanced age, recent emergency surgery, most recent discharge from hospital, the early morning timing of the call for help.'

With regard to the lack of prompt action the following day, the conclusion was that there were shortcomings in communication between the surgery and the on-call service:

'The layout and modes of transmission of the two key documents failed to signal the fraught nature of the problem in a clear enough and timely manner.'

There were eight recommendations following the investigation. In addition to the above, the panel noted the length of and unnecessarily complex internal enquiry that preceded the hearing. They recommended that the PCT:

'carry out a review with colleague NHS organisations into the management and transmission of inter- and intra- organisational post. The management of the complaint prior to the review was attenuated by both routing and clerical delays.'

A concluding comment in the 40-page final report said it all:

<u>*'This service seems to be organised for the benefit of the providers rather than the service users.'*</u>

The Chief Executive of the PCT wrote to say that

- re-organisation the following autumn would attempt to address such issues, especially communication between on-call services and GP practices.
- the provision of on-call services was being discussed and *'note has been taken of the panel's comments.'*

My mother's GP reported that the system regarding incoming information from the on-call service was being reviewed. The doctors would be informed of any faxes in the morning before surgery rather than a message being put in the visit book for attention after morning surgery. She admitted that she would have rung earlier had she known the circumstances, and therefore *'speeded up the admission process.'*

Mum's 80th birthday with the family in Porthcawl, December 1993

The NHS

The course of my complaint against the NHS Trust in relation to my mother's care in the general hospital, was even more protracted and stressful, taking a lot of time, energy and commitment and no doubt again costing the NHS in financial and other ways. The first stage of the process at this time was called the 'local resolution', entirely carried out in-house and remaining largely unresolved from my point of view between June 2003 and September 2004. At that point I asked for an independent review, the outcome also remaining unsatisfactory, after which I referred my case to the Healthcare Commission.

I finally decided that no more could be achieved, having brought about some minor if significant reforms including changes in practice and policy, by September 2006. Between June 2003 and September 2006 I had written fourteen letters to the Patient Liaison and Advice Service (PALS), ten to the Healthcare Commission, two to the Convener of the so-called Independent Review. In total I received twenty-nine letters and three reports from the Trust.

The local resolution stage

I began by raising these issues:

- the unhygienic conditions in the 'isolation' room;
- the questionable decision to move an acutely ill and highly infectious elderly patient to a rehabilitation ward specialising in head injury;
- the failure to address and take action against the risk of thrombosis;
- lack of confidence, competence and supervision of junior medical staff and of communication between staff and myself;
- my mother's reports of rough insensitive handling by night staff;
- the inadequate staffing levels and apparent low morale which may have contributed overall.

I was told that

- the problems with the cleaning service were 'being addressed',
- the staff on the rehabilitation ward were well able to care for my mother,
- the junior medical staff had been well supervised and
- there were clinical reasons for the problems with the drip.
- any precautions against thrombosis had not been appropriate at the time;
- medication would have been dangerous for someone in my mother's condition and people in general did not like wearing compression stockings (Mum having been fully cooperative about this at The Haven),
- the consultant in charge (who was never in evidence) agreed that the junior doctors were accurate in their diagnosis that the vomiting of blood was due to 'coughing'.

There were apologies (which was gratifying) for the unhygienic conditions and the *'significant communication failures'*, and an admission that the service was pressurised. Otherwise it was their word against mine (and my mother's). I was informed that there had been a *'well-documented assessment and care plan'* and that *'the overall standard of nursing care appears good'*.

The independent review

Independent reviews require the appointment of various personnel external to the Trust. By May 2004 there had been no movement on the appointment of an independent nursing adviser, although a lay chairperson/convener had been located, a retired Air Vice Marshall. At this point PALS suggested that the role of the <u>'independent'</u> nurse advisor could be taken by someone <u>from within the same hospital</u>. I was aghast of course, and refused permission. Within two weeks an adviser from another Trust had miraculously been found. The reports from these advisors plus an independent consultant physician reached my desk by August 2004.

The convener apologised *'most profusely for the delays in the resolution of this case'*. His conclusions were that appropriate apologies had been given for the lack of hygienic conditions. He could not find *'any evidence of rough and unsympathetic treatment'* and concluded that the difficulties in fixing the drip were *'not unusual with elderly patients who have had surgery'* – although there had never been an issue with this at The Haven. The nurse adviser though registered concerns:

'that the nursing element of the notes was not as comprehensive or personalised to Mrs. Mill's needs as it might have been….. 'On inspection it is of concern that I can find no record of Mrs. Mill's recent surgery…..My opinion is that this was an extraordinarily relevant omission on the part of the nurses.'

She recommended that:

- this be audited on a regular basis *'to enable standards to be maintained….and allow scope for family members to become involved in agreeing the care of the patient '.*
- *'in view of Mrs. Mill's age, recent surgery and immobility, I consider that at the very least she should have worn compression stockings.'*

The consultant physician dismissed all my concerns. His report seemed biased and judgemental, labelling me as *'an aggressive and difficult'* relative. This was on the basis of the single incident with the auxiliary nurse on the admission ward. I was also blamed for the fact that this nurse afterwards took sick leave. I rather thought that it must have been the last straw that (literally and metaphorically) broke her back, in what was obviously a highly pressurised working environment. There should of course have been two nurses trying to lift my mother.

The accusation prompted a supportive email from my cousin Cyril:

'I find that comment absolutely outrageous. He infers that you are the cause of a nurse being off work for 11 months. Dr. M. states his independence but makes not the slightest effort to enquire further about the alleged rudeness, the nurse herself, her track record or her suitability to be a nurse or what she has been doing for the previous 11 months. Instead he concludes that there was 'clear evidence that Mrs. Elliot because of her emotional distress was, at times, a difficult relative to deal with.' With such evidence of a totally biased attitude it is difficult to accept the independence of his later medical assessments and I am just surprised that the Air Vice-Marshall did not seek further clarification of some of his observations. I mean his whole paragraph about administering the drip seems incomprehensible from my recollections of what you described actually took place. In conclusion it would be fair to say that Dr. M. is perfectly happy with everything in the hospital provided that they always 'apologise appropriately'. I doubt if one person in a thousand can accept criticism without trying to make some form of excuse or justification. If that person is additionally insecure as a result of incompetence, there is always a tendency to lash out. Some responsibility for the dirty ward for example was down to the ward sister and one way to deflect criticism was to accuse you of aggressive or rude behaviour. It is as simple as that and you should put it out of your mind immediately. It has no further validity.'

~

In December 2004 I had another letter from PALS, informing me that the complaint had been passed back to the Trust for another 'local resolution'. In the same letter, and in response to my confusion about the complexity of the complaints' process, I was informed that the so-called independent review was in fact just *'a paper exercise'* – therefore that all the findings had been based on clinical records and reports. Again it was acknowledged that the delays *'have been unacceptable.'*

The Healthcare Commission

In frustration I referred my case to the Commission which had been established in 2004 after the reorganisation of the Care Standards Commission. By the end of August 2006 I had received sixteen items of correspondence from three different case workers.

The first stage was a review by the Complaints Investigation Team. It took nearly a year for all the relevant documentation such as medical records and reports to be received. There were apologies for the delay. I was told that the normal volume of requests in previous years had been 3000, but that since the establishment of the Commission the expected number in the first year alone was estimated to be 9000. In April 2005 I received another apologetic letter with a request for documentation, plus a data protection form and form of application to request an independent review (papers which I had in fact already sent.)

By September I finally heard from a case manager who was reviewing all the information and who intended to refer to a clinical adviser. Although I was still not intending to take legal action, had I wanted to do so, I would by now be concerned, as we were six months from the three-year statutory deadline.

By January 2006 reports from independent advisers had at long last been received:

'On review of the clinical records, it is evident that a full nursing assessment and subsequent care planning did not take place until 3 days after admission….a full assessment should have been documented sooner…Appropriate care plans were implemented, but again there was significant delay…the quality and level of information documented is variable….Observations are recorded regularly but not always in full….pain scores have not been recorded…There is only one fluid balance chart...the standard of completion of both charts is poor….She was referred to a dietician on 05/06/03 but it is not clear from the notes whether she was seen prior to her death…..There is no precise time documented for the re-siting of the venflon' (the drip).

A consultant surgeon concurred with my position regarding the suggestion that an independent clinical adviser be appointed internally during the local resolution stage: *'I share the complainant's concerns'.* He backed the argument by quoting from the Scottish Intercollegiate Guideline Network. He also stated that:

'The Trust did not take adequate precautions against the risk of thrombosis…. Prophylaxis treatment would have been entirely appropriate and that at the very least your mother should have worn compression stockings….: 'medical patients who are immobilised in hospital due to acute illness, especially those with heart failure, infection, diabetic coma, inflammatory bowel disease, nephritic syndrome…The Trust should as a matter of importance have a policy on thromboprophyllaxis that applies across all specialities, and its implementation/adherence audited….'

The case manager instructed the Trust to implement the latter policy and to ensure that adherence to it would be audited. She also made recommendations suggesting that staff be

'reminded of the importance of accurate record keeping in terms of contact details and keeping relatives updated'….better communication between staff and patients, relatives and carers should be in place regarding the reasons for admission or transfer to a particular ward.'

With regard to the length of time it had taken the Trust to complete their so-called independent review, she gave instructions to *'set out what action has been taken or is planned to reduce delays in resolving complaints'* and that where an independent clinical adviser was required to compile a report, *'to ensure that the adviser is in a different geographical location in order to ensure the independence of the advice provided.'*

No action could be taken with regard to the allegation of rough treatment by night staff, accepting a statement from the staff nurse on duty: *'staff did their best to make your mother as comfortable as possible.'* I imagine that it was highly unlikely that any dissatisfaction on the part of a patient – and especially an elderly patient – would actually be recorded in the case notes. Again it was their word against hers.

One of the issues I had discussed with the manager at the PALS service was the importance of admitting mistakes. At the very start of the crisis I had been respectful of the surgeon's apology and never shown any indication either then or throughout the whole period, of an intention to sue either of the three organisations involved. I was of course aware of the underlying agenda in relation to the possible financial risk involved. I was gratified therefore to receive this last letter from PALS:

'I very much appreciate your sentiments with regard to the importance of apologies and thought you might be interested to hear that I have recently implemented a policy known as 'Being Open' – encouraging staff and giving them authority to offer apologies where appropriate as near to the events giving rise for concern as possible.'

~

Having had time to step back and reflect on the whole episode, I tried to understand some of the underlying organisational issues. It had become clear for example in my final conversation with the sister on the elderly ward, that the new emphasis on targets, 'performance indicators', had left staff burdened with paper work to the detriment of direct care. But I suspected that there was more to it than that, remaining as mindful as I could in the circumstances, of the difficult working conditions for all health care employees. I wrote to my local (Labour) MP describing what had taken place and the process of the three complaints.

He replied saying that the NHS was being blamed for problems in the private sector but he could not say whether the poor standards of care in the NHS were due to a *'management or policy failure,'* He pointed to

'recurring problems within the NHS about the status of GPs. They who are not NHS employees fight fiercely to retain their professional independence from prescriptive regulations.'

His government was now faced with the arduous task of

'changing monolithic management, professional and working cultures' and that this *'takes years, but no amount of change or money will ever be able to entirely factor out systems and individual failure.'*

He felt that problems in the NHS and social care were due to years of underinvestment, plus coping with an ageing population which

'lives longer, has higher expectations and which wants access to the latest treatments. This puts a strain on NHS spending that no government will ever be able to fund to the level that would meet all these more recent demands.'

I responded with:

*'I continue to feel appalled that this government has not been able to address issues in relation to what amounts to **very basic care**. We who have supported the Party appreciate the issues created by the previous administration's privatisation policies. These have in our opinion resulted in a mess at all levels: health, social care, transport, education, and other services, where fragmentation has significantly eroded the value base which should underpin such services.'*

So 20 years on………????

Although I was gratified to think that a number of minor if significant positive changes had been made, I realised that not one single person had been disciplined in the whole sorry affair.

~

With Auntie Gwen and Mum outside their house in Porthcawl

White Ash in the Wind: handling the 'absurd aftermath'

Walking the Waves

*Behind us nestle the Welsh hills. In their arms, we paddle gently
through soft waves, peering at toes. There's a low tide,
the sea is shallow, a lake for an ocean. I look now
at the silhouettes in sepia. You're in front, I'm behind,
we make a neat diagonal. Your wire hair's streaked with grey,
your body curved from childbirth, rounder than remembered.
My six-year straightness holds life's hope. We are three years
beyond bereavement, lying as it does on a distant horizon
in smoke-filled city air. Other pictures come to mind:
a two-piece suit in green, the red coat, pink mac,
peach suit at my wedding, those stargazer lilies.*

*Then I see your white ash dissolving in the wind,
a crazy west-coast sunset bleeding into rocks,
the brown plastic of the cheap urn.*

~

After three years I accepted that the process had reached its conclusion, and I was in any case exhausted. Although I have no regrets, I was perhaps unconsciously delaying the moment when I had to face the enormity of the loss itself. The time and energy spent on the work had no doubt delayed the so-called grieving process. In the September of 2006 James and I finally gave ourselves a holiday in Brittany. To date my tears had been shed in anger and frustration. Then something broke inside.

We were walking along one of the magnificent beaches in an almost deserted estuary at low tide, James at some distance from me, probably preoccupied with bird watching. The huge expanse, the beauty, the wide sky, all seemed to scoop me up in their arms and I found myself weeping the 'proper' tears of grief. Some early poems materialized during those two weeks, but when I returned home the task of the grieving that I faced hit me like the proverbial ton of bricks. The silence in the house was particularly painful, I even found myself ringing Mum's number to persuade myself that she wasn't actually there.

My previous encounters with loss had also been traumatic, making the prospect of trying to come to terms with Mum's, daunting. But I also knew that

'The tears we do not shed fall back into our soul.'[6] (from Werther's 'Massenet')

---

[6] *From 'Werther', an opera in four acts by Jules Massenet, 1887*

Stones in a Pram

I had dreadful night terrors as a small child, which no one seemed to understand. Not only had I to make sense of the sudden disappearance of my father, a neighbour babysitting me one night, sat on my bed and told me that I had to be *'a good girl, or your mother will go away, too'*. A year after he died I was molested by a paedophile whilst playing with my doll Mary on the common behind our house. Then my best friend Janet (who was, I later discovered, being abused by her father) told me that there were *'monsters under the bed and in the wardrobe'*.

~

Mary

A sudden memory of wheeling my doll
on a summer morning,
silently wishing for a frilly sunshade.
But maybe we couldn't quite stretch to it.

Then after you died, leaving her out in the rain
so that her body rotted: the head hairless,
one eye blue, the other purple, a fractured eyelid.

I put stones in the pram.

An old arthritic aunt restored her to life
with stuffed fabric: arms, legs, torso.
She's in the attic gathering dust
in her torn pink dress.

Occasionally I go up to say hello.

~

When the time came for me to go to school, a new set of fears emerged. Would my mother still be there at the end of a day? How could I manage all those new relationships? What would happen to me away from the (comparative) safety of home? I became school phobic, so appalled at the prospect that I screamed all the way to the school gates. Eventually my stressed mother enlisted the help of a relative to take over the task of dragging me there.

I was aware too that my mother was not well. She took me on visits to her GP: a warm, caring Scot called Dr. Gray, who gave me sweets in test tubes from her desk drawer, whilst she and Mum had half-whispered conversations. I guess there were tears too, adding to my bewilderment. During this first seven-year period, (crucial as we now know to healthy adult development), we were very poor, my mother trying to survive financially on a meagre widow's pension plus rent from our various lodgers. Privacy was another factor: we shared our three-bedroomed terraced house with two other families, a model of living that was to follow us when we moved back to Wales. For many years afterwards we lived with my Aunt Victoria, a music teacher, her husband William, and my mother's divorced brother Rees.

Thankfully, though, there were many positives: my mother's determination; our love for each other; the support from family, especially Auntie Gwen, who was at the time working as a hospital sister nearby in Clapham, so 'available' both physically and psychologically; my paternal grandparents, grieving as they were too. Eventually I had help conquering my fears about school, in the form of a kind and gentle 'lollipop' man who sat chatting with me under a lovely old oak tree in the school playground. He gradually enabled me to feel confident enough to join the other children in the classroom, where I discovered the wonder of learning. Maybe the tree also played a part.

I survived…

~

Growing up subsequently in Porthcawl was wonderful: bracing sea air, walks, picking daffodils in the woods, mushrooms at dawn, fun with the family - picnics, playing cards, fish and chips from newspapers in our old caravan, loads of presents at Christmas. I was given every advantage under the sun.

Uncle William pitching the tent at Ogmore-by-Sea, a favourite beauty spot of ours. Mum in the centre, me larking about, Auntie Vic in front trying to keep the peace!

At school I made good friends despite a degree of bullying. Some children clearly saw me as a bit odd and I also sensed my 'difference': I had no brothers or sisters, an English accent, no father.

There is one vivid memory of a chemistry lesson when I was just eleven. Mr. Llewellyn, another kindly fellow, was asking round the class what our fathers did. To this day I'm not sure of the purpose of the exercise, how it related to the science. Or even if it was appropriate. I remember how my whole body seemed to seize up and of desperately crossing my fingers hidden in my lap, not to be put on the spot. How did I feel? Terrified and ashamed. It was all my fault. Thankfully the lesson bell rang in time before it was my turn.

Whilst we were all thrilled when Mum established her bakery, for me it meant that she was never home when my school day finished. My auntie was always teaching the piano in the front room of our house and Uncle William usually engrossed in something on the TV or else napping. So when I hadn't stayed behind at school for various activities, I had a solitary tea and then retreated to my bedroom to do my homework. When Mum came home from her shop – in the early days after she had been scrubbing the place on hands and knees - she was exhausted, and would collapse in front of the television. Having a bakery means, as bakers will know, a very early start to heat up ovens and prepare everything to sell by opening time. So early nights were also the order of each day. This lack of time together with little opportunity to talk, although by no means her fault, meant that our relationship was not nourished in the normal way. I had to bottle up all the difficult feelings any child growing up will experience, in addition to the distress caused by bullying. She was anyway completely unaware of the latter.

In school I was aware of another kind of pressure. I now felt I had to please my mother by 'doing well', it would make her happy. I was successful, always coming near the top of the class, but it was at a cost, even though I loved learning. During the build-up towards my 'A' levels, I stopped eating school dinners, finding the mayhem of canteen-eating amongst hordes of noisy children unbearable. I found I couldn't lift the food to my mouth without shaking uncontrollably. My wonderful best friend Margaret stepped in and wrote to my mother, who now recognized how much I needed her, and came home early in time to be with me and make my tea. She stayed around too whilst I quietly studied.

~

Fast forward to my time at university and other experiences of loss, the nature of which held a complexity of their own, building on the feelings with which I was still unconsciously grappling.

I had gained a place to read English at Royal Holloway College in Surrey, which meant that I was near to my grandparents. My relationship with my Grandma had always been close, but now I had opinions of my own. During one visit we had our first 'words', although what the argument was about is lost. Her last remark, hinting at disappointment in me, stung me to the core:

'My, how you've changed'.

The next time I saw her, she was lying semi-conscious in the downstairs freezing cold 'parlour' having contracted flu and refusing to call a doctor. This was a pattern adopted since the death of her son, when she had become socially phobic and a virtual recluse. Gran had also developed a dreadful skin complaint which made her sensitive to heat and meant that the house was perpetually cold. Although there were times when she had been great fun, essentially she had never moved beyond her own bereavement, having idolized her only child.

So the above words, with their residue of blame, stayed with me, hovered in the air as I later watched her writhing in a hospital bed, the virus having turned to pneumonia. As she was dying she shouted for my father, my poor grandfather mistakenly thinking she was asking for him. I still often dream of their little house, in which I had stayed so often as a child, wander through the rooms, smell that particular aroma when the front door opened to a warm welcome.

Small House

*I loved to poke fingers into snapdragons to see if they would bite,
remember a sensation of purple velvet, the same colour
as Grandma's clothes in the wardrobe, with stout shoes
for legs grown thick. In the hallway and up the stairs,
bleach melted with polished lino, moth balls,
and the faint whiff of spent coal.*

*In the front parlour where no one parleyed,
I played 'Invitation to the Dance' on the gritty piano,
daring to challenge the silent curse. On the sofa
like an open coffin I read about Topsy
and grieved for the cruel world.*

*Grandma's old bandages trailed from her raw fingers,
but in the morning sunlight of the neat garden
she would brush her long hair that cascaded
down her strong back like a silver waterfall
and throw dead ends to the unsuspecting birds.*

*She ironed with the flex plugged in the light,
scrubbed clothes with the washboard,
made mouth-melting pastry on the same table
where on a Sunday evening Grandpa polished shoes.*

*Milk was kept in a bowl of cold water in the sink,
never curdled. The milkman came with orange juice
that tasted like nectar.*

*In the morning Grandpa brought tea so strong
as to stand your spoon. I would wait and pour it away,
not to hurt his feelings.*

*The bed was like sleeping on molehills,
you had to curve around them.*

*Grandpa grew raspberries for pies, peas for the lamb.
He took me to Sainsbury's in the High Street,
where ladies wore white caps and you swished sawdust
as you trod the floor. Cheese and sausages
were wrapped carefully in greaseproof,
placed gently into his old leather bag,
whilst he smiled with glittering eyes as he said:*

'This is my granddaughter'.

*Then suddenly everyone was beaming, as if
the sun had finally come out after a long storm.
For tea we had tinned pilchards, golden syrup
on white bread. When no one was looking
I would steal a mars bar from the tin on the bureau.
Then fart.*

'You've blown orf again!'

*Grandma would laugh, her cheeks
resume the redness I liked to see
when she danced for me, trying to kick
her heavy legs heavenwards.*

'Oh my poor 'ol feet. Cor blimey O'Reilly!'

*We played rummy on the chair seat.
Once she threw my tiddlers down the drain.
They were square stocky folk, never kissed,
held hands or even took pills, but something told me
they might break like fine china if touched.*

*In his shed next to the compost Grandpa repaired old watches.
It was so dark I couldn't work out how he could see, but maybe
he wasn't looking at watches.*

*In the Blitz they would cramp up together
in the cupboard under the stairs,
or if it was safe enough watch the bombs
fall over London from the bridge.
War for them seemed a strange mix
of delight and fear. They rationed themselves
for ever after, made do, never bought a fridge
or a washing machine, not even a twin tub.*

*There were occasional jaunts to brothers
and sisters dispersed across the suburbs;
they were a ruptured generation,
doomed to spend evenings watching Cilla Black
and Sandy Shaw on the small screen,
sleep in lumpy beds under army blankets.*

*He was never mentioned, my Dad: his dead presence
pressed down from the roof like lead.*

Curtains were kept drawn.

My twenties were a not unusual experience: I fell in and out of love, worked and played, travelled, made lifelong friends, got a bit 'lost', changed direction from English teaching to train as a social worker. Then in 1979 Uncle William died.

~

In addition to my grandfather, he had been a kind and loving father figure during my childhood. Most of all, being retired, he was always 'around' for me. Perhaps even more importantly and crucial to my later development, in my feeling so safe in his presence, he had by his example reassured me that not all men were sexual predators. Like my Grandma, he too could be great fun, taking me in his car for jaunts, buying me ice cream and playing games. We had a tent which only he could pitch, then it was tennis against the backdrop of the steelworks at Port Talbot, mountains of sandwiches, cakes and tea from the thermos. In order to delay bedtime, which I still hated, I would snuggle up to him in his armchair, as though we were in a kind of pact together to delay the inevitable moment of facing the isolation and the dark. The scene for this poem is a lovely place called Merthyr Mawr, where as a family we would gather daffodils and primroses in the woods:

For Uncle William

I tramped by torchlight in the damp lane,
with memories like dead daffodils. Then suddenly,
above, through spare branches eaten by winter,
flashed starlight, a sky to die for.
Fireflies twitched, and the moon, like a scythe,
cut through clouds. The darkness was indeed visible.

The dawn poured over walls, pelted with moss.
It was there, from beneath the snowdrops that I felt
a hand gently rise to caress my cheek. I remembered
his softness. At water's edge I saw my elf-child
stalk through sea-grass, pick over stones,
playing hide-and-seek. I wore thoughts, like a forget-me-not haze.

In the morning the crack of a twig, woodpecker-bitten,
a strike of kingfisher blue near water, and in the bark
of a stout tree, saw his creased skin, his white whiskers
through the web of a spider. I remembered evenings,
nuzzling in his lap by the fire. In the young light,
felt the blanket of affection, and in the early mist, a kiss.

~

As I approached adolescence, our relationship started to feel a bit different, maybe not unusual; that creeping sense of detachment from 'childish' things. Then my mother dropped what constituted a bombshell:

'It's about time you realised what he's really like!'

I knew that he was always watching us to ensure we switched off unnecessary lights or electric fires; that he had chocolates in a cupboard that he never shared; that he got agitated and angry when losing at cards. But now there seemed to be another problem - the fraught relationship between him and my mother.

There was a quarrel over money. What else? Mum paid her way in the house, with Uncle keeping a close watch on bills and ensuring that they exchanged signed receipts. One day he accused her of forging his signature. I as a 13 year-old was witness to a horrifying exchange of curses. As my mother fled the room within which I was trapped, he shouted:

'I'll murder her!'

Where all this insane anger came from I will never really know, but what I do suspect is that somewhere along the lines an underlying sexual repression played a part. Anyway, my mother lived on, but whereas I had enjoyed such simple relationships with both of them, now my loyalty was torn apart. Leaving home for university was a relief as well as a wrench, but subsequent visits were characterised by a painful unease. Then he contracted prostate cancer and my early sense of powerlessness returned. One memory is of him sitting in the corner of the lounge, alone, tears silently coursing down his cheeks. The last time I saw him, he was being carried clumsily down the curved staircase to the sound of his cries.

At the funeral service, I had my first ever panic attack, then became, unlike his wife or indeed anyone else, distraught. At least I was able this time to show how upset I was. No one really knew how to comfort me.

'Oh, don't upset yourself, Uncle William wouldn't want that!' admonished his un-tearful wife.

I was at the time in the middle of social work training at Chelsea College, living in my own flat in Streatham. During the winter, waiting in the cold for the bus to Sloane Square, I started to experience a sharp vaginal pain. Initially I thought it was the after-effect of an attack of cystitis, to which I was prone. When the pain continued through the winter, and after a number of different investigations which could locate nothing organically wrong, I realised that maybe I needed psychological help and persuaded my GP to refer me. Only very recently I read that this kind of psychosomatic pain may be indicative of buried anger…

The therapy was intense, a psycho-analytic approach, two sessions weekly. After a few months it felt pointless: I was still in pain and frightened of breaking down, so was holding back in the sessions, which in themselves felt terrifying. The therapist eventually said she felt the work wasn't achieving anything. It felt like another bombshell, as if I had failed her, rather than the opposite. I had also by this time, despite my fear, formed some degree of trust in the relationship. Not only that, I didn't know where else to go, and at least I felt she cared about me.

That Christmas I went home to Wales where my mother saw I wasn't well. I couldn't disclose what was going on for me; I had at all costs to protect her. So I blamed it on the social work training which was in reality also challenging, although somehow I was successfully completing assignments and getting through various placements. In fact during this period I feel to this day I was doing some of my best work. So something was working…

With the New Year came a new me. I broke down in the sessions and bared my soul. The physical pain vanished. My memory is of weeping for a whole year afterwards: for my Dad, for my Uncle, for Grandma, for my Mum. We worked hard together for another two years, during which time I gained new insights which have since served me in good stead. Not long after the therapy ended, I met and married my wonderful husband James. Then Grandpa died.

~

He had sold his house and moved in with my mother a few years after being widowed, but appeared not to be coping with living in our family. There were more rows, thankfully not witnessed by me, although again I felt pulled in all directions. One day, at the age of 86 he 'ran away' to live with his sister-in-law in Hampshire, leaving my mother's photograph under the mattress, the glass shattered where presumably he had stamped on it. It was hard to imagine this mild-mannered man in such anger. This time though my mother was concerned that I should keep in touch with him, and I was in any case unprepared to have yet another of my precious relationships undermined.

Subsequently on a Sunday, Grandpa and I would meet under the clock at Waterloo station and enjoy outings in the city, where he would take me out to lunch followed usually by an afternoon concert at the Queen Elizabeth Hall. The quarrel was never mentioned, and he always asked after my mother. Eventually he developed Alzheimer's, finally dying of stomach cancer at the age of 92.

My last memory of him is grim. I continued to visit, even though he no longer knew me. In itself this was a source of anguish, as anyone with relatives suffering the condition will know. Then I was left to organise the funeral, this time allowing myself to grieve openly and without reservation: it helped maybe that I was the only member of my family present, my mother being preoccupied at the time with the last illness of her sister Victoria. Often in my dreams I have seen him all alone in his little house, then at daybreak, waking up to the equally painful realization that he is no longer here. Being preoccupied in sorting out his affairs meant that I couldn't attend Auntie's funeral to say goodbye to her, so I have her photo above my piano. I often ask her for guidance when I am learning a new piece. Music reunites us.

~

Years later I took part in a community group in the Art gallery in York, helping to set up an exhibition called *'Reflections on War',* where I found myself immersed in writing poems on the subject. Grandpa was gassed twice at the battle of Ypres in the Great War.

At Ypres

So, Grandpa, what did you do at Wipers?
Was it fun? Could you swim in the sea?
Did you ride the donkeys, go to the fair?
Have parties? Joke with friends?

Drive your little car down summer lanes
smelling sweet with wild honeysuckle,
violets, bees sucking pollen, clouds
drifting gently towards England?

Why do you call it Wipers?
Is it why your eyes water? Or that
all the laughter brings tears of joy!
Sing to me again – that song - to

pack up my troubles in an old kit bag
and smile! Will you buy me one?
I would smile too, seeing you remember
the happy times, away from London grime,

a break from work, fresh air, good food,
the company of men. They'll meet you
there again someday, just like that other song!
Can I come too next time?

I also tried to imagine my grandmother's feelings during that period:

The Home Fire

I kept it burning. Each night, baby asleep, watched flames
like the waves of your hair; heaped on coals
we could ill afford. Fire and love survived,
for our child, born so soon, was of a passion
I never thought to own. It seemed we three would be so happy.

In the autumn I planted bulbs. With stubby fingers
he tried to help, delighted in soil warmed by summer;
peered at worms, entranced by sunshine playing on leaves,
the shape of clouds, soft breath of a garden ready for sleep.
The light caught the cream of his new skin.

In winter, I felt desire re-kindle. Sometimes though,
when the coals hissed, wood crackled,
sending sparks skywards, I heard battle.

At last, in blue crepe, a new hat with feathers,
our boy sailor-suited, his hand clasped tight,
we paced the platform, treading light.

Then wheezing steam, the train emerged
through morning mist. I saw ash faces
peer through smoky glass, then picked out yours.

As we kissed, a low gurgle came from your throat;
strangled sentences, platitudes.

We turned to our son, an excuse not to talk.
At supper, I mistook the tears for relief.
On your lap, the boy's head glistened.

'It's the gas' you said. 'I was gassed.'
The embers sank. I stared whilst your chest heaved.

~

In 2001 Auntie Gwen began to show signs of agitation, being preoccupied with worries about her finances, despite my reassurances. She had suffered with high blood pressure for some time and these concerns were no doubt contributing. One Sunday afternoon she became delirious; a young locum GP diagnosed a chest infection and prescribed antibiotics.

During the next 24 hours she kept falling out of bed, after which another call to the surgery prompted a visit by the regular GP who immediately diagnosed a major stroke. Auntie was rushed to hospital and admitted to the same ward where my mother was to die two years later. I travelled south to find the latter exhausted. On the ward, we discovered Auntie writhing in a cot jammed up against a wall. She was badly bruised down one side of her body where she had launched herself against the brickwork, having had several more strokes. She was now blind as well as unable to speak coherently. I went to find help to ask if she could be made more comfortable, to be told by a rather grumpy male staff nurse that he was on his break and would *'come in 20 minutes.'*

~

Auntie had started to train as a nurse at the age of 18 in 1927, in a small fever hospital in Chippenham, before moving to London to work in five more, as a general nurse, fever nurse, and midwife. During WW2 she stayed faithfully at her post all the way through the conflict, keeping a diary which we subsequently donated to the Imperial War Museum. It was later to be used in a television documentary in which she was interviewed, talking about her experiences. In her 80's she wrote a nursing memoir which I edited and published during the pandemic, feeling that there were valuable lessons to be learned, especially in relation to the organisation of services dealing with major infections.

Now here was my wonderful aunt, thrashing around in distress, with few to appreciate what had been her unique contribution to the profession. I couldn't help reflecting on how many dying patients she had in turn sat with and made comfortable in their last moments. I felt pulled apart, wanting to be with her, but also responsible for my mother who was finding the visits intolerable. Yet there is one last consoling memory of her reaching out to stroke my cheek, smiling and trying to say my name. Later she died alone.

It was against this backdrop of loss that I approached the new task of mourning my mother, feeling as though some dramatic script had already been written for me. Now here I was, going on stage for the umpteenth time.

~

The Single Tree in the Rainforest

Returning to York in 2003 after Mum's funeral, I was plagued with flashbacks and nightmares, and as described, aware of a deafening silence. Disposing of my mother's belongings, especially her clothes, had been painful. I found myself unable to part with a little pink raincoat, which I kept in my wardrobe, periodically taking it out to savour the familiar smell of her, which still lingered.

Raincoat

It was not for some time after
that I thought to look in the pockets:
a final Tesco bill for
two apples,
a few bananas,
a pint of milk.

Was it war-born caution,
or simply all you could carry?

I contemplated dry-clean,
but couldn't part with the smell:
the memory of my butterfly mother
in pink polyester.

~

My career had developed over the years; by this time I was employed in social work education. In the summer of 2005 the funding for my academic work was withdrawn and I needed to think about alternative employment, although at nearly 55 this would be difficult. Quite by chance I saw an advert for a caseworker in the newly established Independent Complaints Advocacy Service, where I was successful in gaining a post. Over the following year I was involved in helping a number of people, some of whose stories were much more shocking than ours, with the system remaining so difficult to navigate and underpinned always by political agendas. A year or so later I was made redundant when the service was transferred to another provider, probably a blessing in disguise, in that together with the end of the enquiry, it freed me to start in earnest on the real work of grieving.

I frantically busied myself with the garden, needing to make something grow, whilst applying half-heartedly, and without success, for other jobs. Two years later I decided to train as a volunteer for Cruse Bereavement Care. A few weeks before I was due to start the course, our beautiful old cat Flossie had to be put down after struggling with a protracted and distressing illness. As anyone with a pet knows, a significant bereavement too.

As I went through the training, I started to feel overwhelmed. In preparing a portfolio of written work I revisited the multiple bereavements. When asked to take on two clients, I fell into a blind panic, thankfully realising that I was emotionally unsafe to work. It was a terrible shock though, and source of disappointment, to discover that I clearly couldn't 'move on' as I had hoped. My life felt in tatters: no career, no family, and leaving aside James' amazing support, I felt completely at sea. I ached for the comfort of a mother's presence.

The Time of your Child

That time, the time of your child, who in the belonging
was included in games, meals and quarrels; was central,
centred down the drift of years, when the earth somehow stood still,
like a monument, holding at bay those twin towers of Future and Past;
out of focus and in some distant territory. Where on Sundays
the house steamed with roasts and tarts, welsh cakes and tea,
questions and answers, statements and facts, idle gossip
about this and that - the sermon, Mrs. Jones' hat.

Where at night, tucked beneath orange blankets, I would listen
to horns in fog, snuggling in the knowledge of the misty sea,
moonshine in valleys. On crisp mornings, ice on windows,
huge fires at evening, polished coal in small hills on pavements.
Took delight in toes that tingled, telling of the hearth, where we
toasted pikelets and boiled black kettles. I was shrouded in love.

In the spring picked primroses in woods dense with daffodils,
enough to fill the house, They threw sunshine for weeks.
In summer, pitched camp at Kenfig, picked purple dewberries,
waded through sandwich mountains, tea from the thermos,
played our version of tennis where no one lost. Or at Trecco
ate fat-drowned chips in the caravan which never went anywhere,
but that was ok, we were happy to stay. Perched on soft knees,
kissing whiskers, we had a secret bedtime tryst to stay up late,
played cards on the Sabbath: ('What would mother think?')
Cheated, won halfpennies and farthings, stole chocolate, was scolded,

but not too much or too often. We laughed at cakes that turned upside-down,
at daft presents at Christmas, sang and danced, hymns round the piano;
uncles into princes, aunties to queens. In our playing I was deceived
to think of you as mates; we would grow together, never stop eating chips
by the sea, hearing embers softly hiss at twilight. A force pulled us backwards
like a wayward wind to childhood, then back and forth between two spheres
of time. We were children, non-children, floated between work and idleness,
surprised to feel the gap widen. We all needed parents, were as lost as Pan.

Now there is cracked marble, weeds growing through gravel,
names and dates which grow dim, stones tipsy with neglect.
I am left: the last in the queue at the bus stop, the only bear on the ice floe,
the single tree in the rainforest, the final chord of the concerto.
In what strange place and time have I found myself, as if transported by tardis
to a non-place, non-time, neither old nor young, but not that smiling child.
Unsafe in this new frequency, I drift through unmarked years.

~

There were the usual 'symptoms' of grief: hearing Mum's voice, feeling my heart stop momentarily on seeing a physical likeness. I had nightmares about her distorted body, especially having been sent the post-mortem report during the enquiry, containing details of the exact weight and dimensions of her brain and other organs. It was horrible to picture these, her body carved up on a slab. Meantime there was ongoing, if not increasing anxiety, about the influx of major hospital infections, so that the whole episode was never far from my conscious mind. Clostridium Difficile became a more familiar term in general, along with MRSA. Wards faced closure, elderly people were dying from neglect and/or infections alongside the usual maladies of old age. Harold Shipman hit the headlines. The world was fast becoming a very unsafe place; my anxieties galloped away with themselves.

I had a stone erected over Mum's small 'grave' in Porthcawl, having thought long and hard about the wording. It was something 'concrete' to hold on to, albeit being so many miles away, so I took the photo. In the next few years James and

I went back to the cemetery to take flowers, most of which were eaten by the rabbits in the fields behind. Not to be deterred, in subsequent visits I took shells and pebbles collected from the beaches she so loved.

Going back to Wales to 'visit' dead people and childhood haunts brought back many memories, as well as a stark realisation of my isolation. The poems kept coming, the emotional place in which I now found myself, plus the chasm left by relative idleness, was giving space to the expression of tangled feelings. I felt it as nothing short of a miracle, never having written serious poems before. Symbols and images were finding their way to the written page, although as yet I had to understand what they all meant.

As well as the loss of the Welsh family, wounds about my father's early death surfaced. When clearing Mum's flat I had discovered his love letters in an old brown envelope. For the year after she died, I agonised whether to read or destroy them, respecting my parents' privacy. Or could I allow myself a glimpse of the father I had not known? The temptation was too great and one gloomy winter afternoon I sat down and worked my way through.

It was sad indeed, not just for the absence in my life of this sensitive, kind person who had so loved my mother, but also the loss to him of his own life, with all its hopes and dreams. In one letter for example, he had talked about his excitement at the thought of a full family life to come. Using his imagined 'voice' in the poem *'An Unlived Life'* was a novel and cathartic experience, a device with which I continued to play. It had brought me inside his skin. I also tried to imagine what memories might lay buried:

Maybe

I saw you reading
in a corner, under yellow lamplight,
hair still damp from November smog,
or smelt the tweed of your cheap jacket:
stale smoke, a father's sweat.

Maybe heard you whistling in spring
as you upturned soil ready for flowers.
No doubt tasted love in your gaze
as you tucked up sheets, read stories,
full of hope for a future not to be yours

or mine.

I used my work in a training session on childhood bereavement for 'Cruse' and later for the launch of my first poetry collection where two members of the audience came up to me in tears at the end of the evening, saying how much the poems had helped them, as bereaved 'children' themselves. This one, based on an anecdote my cousin told me, and which I wrote in fact only a few years ago, particularly touched them:

Party, March 1953

The child weaves her way through a forest of dark legs,
sees her image reflected in grandfather's shiny shoes,
grandmother's tears. There is strange noise,
not the sort with which birthdays are celebrated;
mother's voice is cracked, not the same one
that sings Welsh lullabies. China cups rattle
on their saucers, trying to secure themselves.

Outside, the smog of March curls around chimney pots
and tries to get in. The child coughs. Someone picks her up
in their strong arms. Poor little mite, they say. Their breath
smells of sherry and there are crumbs on their clothes
from the cakes her mother made last night in a frenzy of cooking.

It will take time, says another, but the child will be a blessing,
a comfort. The child will help.

The child wonders how and why she must help her mother.
After all, she is never allowed in the kitchen. Undaunted,
her curiosity in permanent flow, she tugs at the grey skirt,
asks if it's someone's birthday. She is hushed and shushed,
the wheezing sounds like the cold draught under the door.
Already in her tiny mind she senses an unclear transgression,
worse than the worms she dug up in the garden; the coal
she smeared over her white dress on Sunday morning;
the incessant chatter that gives everyone a headache.

She will bury this time at the back of her garden
where nothing but weeds grow under the pear tree.
The other time too, that long dark night,
when her screaming mother squeezed her so tight
she couldn't breathe, will lie in stagnant water after rain.

Instead she will search endlessly: in the arms of lovers,
the poignant notes of a Nocturne, in poems and stories,

*in the sea, in the sunset, in the smell of a jacket.
She will stare at the photographs, daring him to speak;
scrutinise his eyes for any message, good or bad;
even feel desire in his slim body, the way he holds
that cigarette, the calm with which he stands like a star,
gazing into some distant space. She will devour his books,
knowing he has held the pages in his gentle hands.
Finding she agrees with an occasional faint scribble
written hastily in a margin, is a small miracle.*

*Otherwise, all she has is a lock of baby hair,
a brown leather wallet with his last train ticket,
a crumpled ten shilling note, unspent.*

*Everything afterwards will be un - something:
unlived, unloved, unheard, unfelt, unshared.
Even his resting place is unmarked.*

*All leavings, partings and endings will make her breath uneven,
give her an ache in her side, send her back somewhere
into that tangled undergrowth of black suits and grey skirts
and the shiny shoes of her grandfather.*

*But in these moments she will endeavour to remember
the sight of that rainbow arching over the graves,
when she once searched fruitlessly for his.*

One of the very few photos of me with both parents

One year I had to go down to London for an eye appointment, staying with James in a hotel on the Chelsea Embankment. Instead of doing much sightseeing, we spent a great deal of time, along with thousands of other silent bystanders, watching a poor stranded whale. It was an extraordinary weekend; thousands of us linked with this tortured creature:

The Whale in the Thames

A huge body, battered and stranded amongst grey rocks and plastic,
Pokes its bottled nose in tarred pebbles, hears only the clicks of cameras,

hours chime, the hushed whispers of children on shoulders, the faint kisses
of lovers, and the soft slow hiss of the tide as it rises and falls, sucking life.

Gently curious, she craves company, has squirmed through unfamiliar spaces
between bridges, nets and boats, like a massive eel sifting through debris.

But riding the shallow bed, she bleeds. Unnoticed, the blood seeps
past tourists. We watch. The sun picks out the green and gold of the bridge.

At first they use fear to drive her back. There is something obscene
in her nakedness, the floundering in shallows, the ring of men,

the silent caress of a waiting world. I exchange pleasantries,
all the while with one eye on wave, following grey flesh.

In the park birds sit, respectfully quiet. Time passes.

She has moved out of sight, thrashes in some silent place,
beyond banks and locks. Next day, at water's edge,

teeth are gritted as cranes poise, itching to lift. We feel
her terror pierce the sunshine. But neither Science nor Logic

can wrench her to safety. Now she is bone, washed white, on show,
a faded headline, a memory, as once again
we watch the brown river run softly to song's end.

~

At the end of winter, we tend to get a number of old bees taking refuge in our conservatory. I always try to help them back outside in the hope that they will somehow find a new lease of life:

I was about to sit down to papers:
news of ash clouds and elections,
planes grounded like wounded birds on tarmac,
climate change and wars on foreign soil.

Spring, though early, seemed late.
We had cleared the remnants of winter,
searched for buds amongst dead foliage,
a new leaf here and there.

I glanced down, saw you struggle across red tiles,
how you tottered sideways like an old orange man,
brought you out into sunshine with glass and card.
Watched tiny legs tremble in the evening air,

eased you into flower, where you clambered clumsily;
it glittered with recent rain. Thought you could feast
on pollen and water, revive and fly. Ageing limbs
explored alien territory, imagined recovery.

Later I turned leaves gently over
to find you hunched in the curve of death.

It seemed that I was forever trying to stop everything from dying, feeling such anguish watching these creatures gasping for life. The subject of the sunflower in the poem previously quoted, had also found its way into a short story I had written. It was clearly potent, though at the time I had no idea what it all 'meant'. Why were these creatures, these images, so important to me; why did I feel so impelled to write about them?

*'A Word is dead when it is said, they say,
I say it just begins to live that day'*

Emily Dickinson

During the time when I was involved with the exhibition at the art gallery, the creative writing tutor leading our group encouraged me to think about developing my style. Looking for more academic guidance, I embarked on an MA degree, which process proved exhilarating and has continued since, via writing workshops and courses. It was a golden opportunity not only to improve my writing, but also to understand it in more depth. My words began to live.

I considered 'Sunflower' in more depth. Superficially, it is about the real plant, but the physical elements then began to emerge as symbolic. The brown earth maybe needs no explanation – *'earth to earth'*? – or more crudely, the physical mess my poor mother was in; my frenzied attempt to tug the dying plant away, my despair at watching life ebb away from her, all colour gone.

The *'breast shaped dent'* must be a reference to the maternal, the close bond between child and mother, and the *'mangled roots'* the sense of being abandoned, without the person whose presence had tied me to the planet. There is something of her ruined hands, in the image of the *'leaves like empty puppets'* and the last verse a reference to what was for me, her untimely death. The need to scatter seeds though, is perhaps hopeful: our love for each other and the treasure trove of memory, survives, alongside my commitment to an existence without her.

~

The Fallow Field

*It had been a long walk: a stunning day of white cliffs,
sunshine, sea breezes, kestrels poised above bleached grass.*

Cows grazed, wheat swayed -

*you get the picture. I only took one
as we'd forgotten the camera,
It's still on my mobile –
a nice shot of a yellow yacht ambling across blue.*

*But what I remember now, in September,
is that fallow field we suddenly came across,
how brown it was, empty even of weeds,*

*how it stretched lazily across a gentle slope,
towards coast, defying colour.*

Initially I thought the image of the fallow field spoke of the sense of emptiness, of nothing in my life moving forward. When I came to re-consider this early poem years later, I saw something more positive. Farmers of course leave fields fallow in order to give the soil a rest, a chance to recover strength before being re-planted: nature's way of healing. Maybe I was trying to remind myself of the importance of this in the grieving process: giving oneself time, accepting the lack of movement as a crucial breathing space. As Laurens Van der Post once said:

'to give the soul a chance to catch up.'

~

Here is a poem written after a walk, when we came upon:

An Ancient Burial Ground

There you lie, side by side, tied together by some strange dying.
Mother, father, daughter, son, an interruption of lives.

I ponder the configuration of dates, puzzled by the possibilities
of your story. Others lie scattered here over lumpy ground,
respectably old.

The skies are big, the fields empty, the landscape compressed.
We walk the back lane, pass one or two with dogs, come upon still water;
it stretches endlessly.

We stop a moment, you with your thoughts of history:
of bargemen and horses and towing of grain,
disuse brought on by progress, the stream calm yet lonely,
left now to life more silent.

Meanwhile in the emptiness and imagined memory
I see faces in the dark slime.

~

Colin Murray Parkes reminds us that alongside the pain is a very real awareness of mortality, which gives way to its partner, acute anxiety: *a 'state of high arousal....and occasionally approaching panic'*.[7] Maybe that last image is one such example.

The loneliness of grief is reflected in the description of the landscape, with the sense of isolation from the other human being, who was clearly in quite another mental space, being interested in the history of canals. There is a sense of being

---
[7] *Parkes, C.M. 1996*

haunted, even an awareness of the spirit world. I also saw a connection between the 'disuse' of the stagnant canal and my loss of purpose. This struggle for meaning is crucial for healthy psychological development:

'at each age we seek, must be able to find, some modicum of meaning congruent with how our minds and understanding have already developed.'[8]

I began to realise that the 'economy' of poetry is the best medium for profound emotion:

'One of the differences between poetry and prose is that poetry is beyond words. Poetry is only there to frame the silence. There is silence between each verse and silence at the end.' [9]

'What's writing really about? It's about trying to take fuller possession of the reality of your life…Poetry is the voice of spirit and imagination and all that is potential, as well as the healing spirit that used to be the privilege of the gods'.[10]

'Poetry can tell us what human beings are. It can tell us why we stumble and fall and how, miraculously, we can stand up.'[11]

'Poetry is a zoo where you keep demons and angels'.[12]

'Poetry helps us to understand common things better…Poetry will not teach us how to live well, but it will incite in us the wish to.'[13]

'Poetry is a way of talking about things that frighten you.'[14]

'Poetry is what makes the invisible appear.'[15]

At first I had been expressing raw feelings of loss, what Seamus Heaney describes as his *'howl of sorrow'*[16]. I wrote a long rambling poem in elegiac style, inspired by a favourite photograph of Mum and me paddling in the sea on the Gower coast. It had helped me keep an 'inner dialogue' with her. Years later I returned to the poem re-shaping it entirely in free verse, letting the symbols speak for themselves. In the traditional elegy

---

[8] *Bettelheim, B. 1991*
[9] *Kellaway, K. 2005*
[10] *Ted Hughes*
[11] *Maya Angelou*
[12] *Les Murray*
[13] *David Constantine*
[14] *Mick Imlah*
[15] *Natalie Sarraute*
[16] *Heaney, S. 1995.*

'the importance of telling a story, of clear memory, is central to the poet's (and the psychotherapist's) mission'[17].

With the subject of war still on my mind, I wrote:

As the Crow Flies

Glancing upwards to monitor rain
I saw a black spot against a grey sky.
I thought at first, it was a floater in my vision.
But it was big and unwieldy

flapping like a torn cloak: a Rorschach test.
Something half-alive and inside out,
thrashing on a wire. Higher up, its mate,
balanced like a dancer, intact, looked for worms.

Here I was travelling home by train, looking through the window to see if I would need my umbrella on arrival. The sight of the tortured creature sent me reeling: suddenly I saw dying soldiers caught on barbed wire, intestines falling out, a hideous image of which I am sure we are all by now familiar. At another level it connected with the way in which I too had felt mutilated, my life all 'inside out'. With the help of my tutor I revised the original draft, preoccupied with telling the story, rather than focusing on the symbols with their core message, and 'less' being 'more'. This had me grappling with questions as to how simple or complex a poem needs to be, whether

'the very inaccessibility of a particular poem – its inherent difficulty – forms an integral part of its power and allure'.[18]

Equally difficult at the time was managing the psychological shift between my private world and a more public arena, sharing the poems in a setting where they would be subject to close critical scrutiny:

'We need to be able both to access and objectify our material....the problem is doing both at the same time' ...'involves creating an internal space, distancing ourselves from ourselves.... so that we are both inside and outside ourselves simultaneously and able to switch back and forth fluidly.' [19]

~

Over the years, I have tried to reach some kind of reconciliation, both with the nature of my mother's dying, and the relationship itself. So-called 'healthy mourning' can eventually lead to a kind of reorganisation of the psyche, a

---

[17] *Holmes, J.1993.*
[18] *Seighart, W.2012*
[19] *Hunt, C. and Sampson, F. 2008*

'rebuilding of a secure inner base.' [20] Research also highlights the notion that a key predisposing factor to prolonged grief is *'a history of excessive dependency'*.[21]

Another factor is ambivalence:

'the relation to the object is no simple one; it is complicated by the conflict due to ambivalence...Countless separate struggles are carried on over the object, in which love and hate contend with each other'.[22] John Bowlby defines this as an *'insecure attachment'*, where there is a *'mixture of feelings, intense love and dependency, fear of rejection, irritability and vigilance'*.[23]

~

I searched for a place between sea and shore,
a rock pool, indifferent to land or water,
where small fish darted and crabs hid behind pebbles.

I searched for a time that belonged not to us,
but to another dimension, not of past nor of present,
where spirits hovered like fireflies at dusk.

I searched for a face that was not yours,
but shared by both: a fusion of feature,
careless of beauty, gazing at falling stars.

Maybe here I am trying to capture something of this: alongside an acknowledgement of our closeness ('a fusion of feature'), there is a longing for a neutral psychological space, where my mother and I could meet on equal terms, something we both often found difficult; where what matters in the last analysis is our common humanity, the 'face' that we share, both physically and symbolically.

So now, after, are you no more than a catch in a song, a pause in the music,
an uneven beat, the soft dropping of rain on tiles? No more than a whisper
behind a half-closed doorway, than the whistle of the wind between rafters,
the shudder of a halting train? That shape on the midnight window,
the cloud blocking the moon, autumn leaves in late sunshine?
The scent of old roses in twilight, the song of the blackbird at dusk,
or are you there in the crying child?

But for now, you are the ache in my side,
the sigh in my throat when I rise on cold mornings.

---

[20] *Holmes, J. 1993*
[21] *ibid*
[22] *Freud, S. 1917.*
[23] *Holmes, J. 1993.*

Alongside trying to express the sheer pain of loss, the depiction of the 'uncanny' relates to a phenomenon that has been defined as *'a disturbing of the familiar'*[24]. Numerous forms are described, including the notion of death as familiar yet unimaginable, as well as the idea of a spirit world. The latter *'unsettles all distinctions between being alive and being dead, the real and the unreal'*. These beliefs link with the unconscious process of becoming involved in a piece of writing, (as a reader or writer), which challenges our sense of what is real or unreal. Writing about a death takes one further into this realm, as after all, one is writing about someone who is now no more than a ghost in one's memory.

Evensong in York Minster

In early twilight crowds thin. Candlelight flickers
on old stone, brown wood, the laughter
of carved monsters. Choirboys
stand to attention, testing breath.
Someone sits close, a whiff of lavender
mixes with incense, then the singing
is of heaven, or what we know of it.

We spin in readings, are asked to pray.
I cannot say the words demanded.

Wide aisles mix sound, a melting pot
of late drunks, the hum of traffic, blackbirds.
The last hymn was her favourite.
My throat croaks, sensing her hand in mine.
I huddle, my chest shudders. After, I walk

past nightlights that pray for the nameless.
Great windows glower, colourless in dark winter,
stones clap to heels, I see dead generations.
Tombs loom; underfoot Romans keep vigil
over silver chalice.

This is the Minster, the city's heart.
By day heaves its shoulders
against hordes who cluck at shouting children,
carry wet umbrellas, take photos, scarcely look.

But now it sighs, immeasurably relieved,
stretches to full height and back again.
Stone vaults yawn. I take comfort
into the chill of the night, savouring song
and the faint scent of lavender.

---

[24] *Bennett, A. and Royle, N. 2009.*

The search for the 'lost object' continued. Mourning itself often seems unreal; trying to 'internalise' what has happened, towards an acceptance of the loss. In creative terms, there is a parallel: I was aware, as I wrote, how the *'literary and the real can seem to merge into each other'* and *'when real everyday life suddenly takes on a disturbingly literary or fictional quality'*.

Certainly the struggles in relation to finding the right words to describe feelings, reflects one of the forms that the uncanny can take: a *'crisis in relation to language'* and something *'beyond language'*. In this poem I am trying to convey *'a sense of trauma as ghostly, as that which comes back again and again, which continues, hauntingly'*.

In an article looking at the impact of exile, the writer records this as closely resembling the infant's experience of *'attachment, separation, and loss'* and applauds the exiles' strength in *'utilising this profound life disruption in the service of expanding the self and enhancing one's creative and symbolic capacities.'*[25]

All this resonated strongly with me. Like the exile, I felt in a *'lonely moment'*. My place in the world, no longer being in the role of daughter or having a career, was disrupted, what I *'once was no longer exists"*. I had to find and adjust to a *'new language'* which would give the *'possibility for growth,'* a *'kind of psychic rebirth'*.

Another paper made links between the actual content of dreams and poetry, both of which are felt to have *'a manifest and latent content, and the ambiguity and multiple imagery of the former may be more readily conveyed by the latter than by other forms of creative expression'*.

Dreaming, like poetry, is seen as:

'an attempt to gain mastery over the original threat', and the mourner *'is attempting to cope… by regressing to an earlier primitive state of incorporative fusion with the mother'*. Contemporary poetry with its *'complexity of words'* is seen as lending itself to *'multiple meanings…and uncertainty of interpretation'*.

By the time Keats was in his early twenties he had lost both parents, his grandmother and his two brothers. He died with the 'family disease' of TB by the age of 25 having completed and published a prodigious body of work where his poetry represented:

'an attempt to work through the grieving process….to externalise the dream….and thereby to restore the lost object'.

His search for beauty is seen as something which:

---

[25] *Hollander, N.C. 1998.*

'would allow him to deal with the abstraction rather than the person in an attempt to cope with the threat of loss'.

I too searched for comfort in this way, in calmer moments finding great solace in nature and in apparently trivial experiences. During my studies I was interested to find this quote:

'This capacity to wonder at trifles…these asides of the spirit, these footnotes in the volume of life, are the highest form of consciousness, and it is in this childishly speculative frame of mind, so different from common sense and logic, that we know the world to be good. The delight of the creative mind is the sway accorded to a seemingly incongruous detail over a seemingly dominant generalisation' [26]

I found myself delighted, if not comforted, by what I would have dismissed before as 'incongruous detail'. Another day whilst walking again on a Brittany beach, we came upon a line in the sand:

Snail

Between dry land and water we found across our path
a long straight furrow etched in sand, not wide.
Curious, we traced the line, coming upon
a single snail, colour of grey granite,
as if carved. We watched at close quarters.

Unfazed, it continued its shifting:
crawled out of anonymity to centre stage,
from oblivion to public glare – to meet perhaps
its final challenge, for seagulls hovered.
Amazed by its sense of purpose,
non-wavering, force of energy,
incaution, at how unfrozen by intellect,
we wished our friend a safe journey and pressed on.

Strange though it may sound, here I was inspired by this tiny creature determined to find its way forwards, ignoring risk. These 'footnotes in the volume of life' are essential to the writing process and to mental health, where *'The movement is from delight to wisdom and not vice versa'*[27]. The *'solitary role of the witness'* is crucial in finding: *'A potent charge inside and behind an image'*.

---

[26] *Nabokov, V. 1982.*
[27] *Heaney, S. 1995.*

Here I contemplated the beauty to be found in simplicity:

The Common Blue

Whoever called you common, whose deep blue
the universe has dipped, who dines
on trefoil, marjoram and thyme, and finds
in roadside verge the thistle and white clover.
Who slowly on low ground, in search
of tenderness, will lay a single egg
on fragile leaf, then sleeps head down in dullness
or at night, and nectaring, rests on fog.

No common thing is she who loves the sun,
who from a slug-like thing of green
is dotted too in brown and red, and feeds her friend
the ant. In turn he offers her a bed
whilst sucking honeydew. Close up, her coat of fur
is soft enough to stroke, and dark her watchful eye.

Even spiders became my friends, seemed to be sending me valuable lessons. Once when I was feeling particularly depressed, this happened:

Emily Speaks

(After Emily Dickinson's poem: 'I'm Nobody! Who are you? 1861)

A sleepless September: I've watched a cobweb spider
weave across my window, catch grubs, grow fat.
Sometimes too, from mid-air, centred on silk, she watches me.
Recently, as the restless month gains strength, she's retreated
to a corner. How sensible simply to take shelter.

It's 4 a.m. My stomach hurts at the thought of another day.
I listen to the red Virginia leaves creep then fall
like blood from an ancient wound. The wind tries to speak.
Reaching for a book, I find the one you gave me:
'New Year 1994 - from James to Sue – cos I love you'.

The cover, faded, yet insufficiently to hide her plain blank stare,
dark dress, calm hands resting on cloth, blackbird eyes.
The page opens at random. I must have read it before.
But this time it smacks of the miraculous. In an unearthly hour
it is Emily who tells me, it's okay to be Nobody, like her.

Using the role of witness helped me to move away from self-indulgence to express empathy, which in itself is healing. From the tsunami in Japan:

Here, the sun now sets,
licks orange fingers across calm water.

Here, where, instead of boats,
there's an old yellow sofa
with no-one to sit on its bright cushions.

Here, where instead of seaweed,
bodies are strewn sideways at the shoreline,
and grow green.

Here, where the waves tremble,
not with the games of children,
but the swaying of cars
taking a nose dive into the deep.

Here, where instead of gulls,
infants wail at twilight,
and men in white coats plod and sift through mud.

…to the children dying in Syria:

Alongside sunshine and seagulls,
shellfish and sandcastles,
eating sandwiches in dunes,
or sipping red wine on the patio,

we see the charred bodies of children.

Whilst we consider our best photographs,
instead the image of a face ripped red, a howling mouth.

It casts a deep shadow over the leaning keep of a castle,
or the glimpse of a heron standing sentinel at dawn.

…drowned refugees:

Lampedusa, October 2013

He lay, face down, spread-eagled:
a dark starfish, cruciform on water,
palms flat, outstretched,
the fish bleeding his black eyes,
whilst his mother wailed, against sounds
of old wood as it thudded on wave.

There was nothing they could do,
save watch him being tipped over
like slops from a bucket into a drain.

Maybe they saw the gulls peck
at his thin clothes, his salt-matted hair,
expose his young spine.

The mid-land sea curved upwards,
folded over. He was lost
amongst oil and plastic,
lead, mercury, phospates,
washings and sewage
from the yachts of the rich.

Then there is also the simple sound and 'feel' of poetry. Julie Kristeva[28] looks at its sheer physicality, believing that

'poetic language links us with the 'semiotic' or pre-linguistic realm of development, especially in the relationship with the mother, through rhythm, sound and bodily feelings: the physicality of poetry'.

Hearing poetry read aloud enhances the written word. With other students during my degree course, I was invited to present some of my work. The last time I had recited a poem was in school: I remember my whole body tingling as an eight-year-old with Blake's 'Tyger'. I suddenly realised how alive the action still made me feel, the process almost constituting a reassurance of my own heartbeat, which of course, I owe to my mother. Moreover, Heaney[29] believes that:

'the intonation of a poem……..stands for the motion of the soul'.

~

---

[28] *Hunt, C. and Sampson, F. 2006*
[29] *Heaney, S. 1995.*

Spikes in your Skull

Clearing

Thousands of them, packed tightly in fat albums:
smiling faces sandwiched between fields, hills,
gardens in summer, woods in winter,
suggesting lives well lived. I decide to rationalise.

It's not so easy, like throwing away your baby shoes,
or those love letters with the purple handwriting,
school reports, grandfather's medals, old diaries,
newspaper cuttings of successes long forgotten.

Here's your mother, looking lovingly out, as if
those words whose spikes still stick in your skull,
had never been spoken.

Those of us lucky enough to have lived long, will more than likely be in possession of hundreds if not thousands of family photos. Some favourites have found a satisfying place in this memoir, the others imprinted into memory. As the poem describes, I had a fit of clearing one day, remembering happy times: birthdays and Christmases, countryside jaunts in the car, meals out, playing cards, singing….

Many years though after Mum's death, when I thought I had reached some kind of closure, memories of difficult scenes between us stubbornly re-emerged. I felt anger rising through the grief, couldn't get some words out of my head. I was also becoming more aware that uneasiness in my relationships with others, especially women, were projections of our difficulties. I became preoccupied with trying to fathom why on occasions she had been hurtful, reflecting at the same time on the part I may have played in what had clearly been her dismay.

Ambivalence is probably one cornerstone of all close relationships, but in the context of grappling with loss it can be especially stressful, when conflicting feelings war with one another. Growing up, as described, all I felt was a deep love, a permanent longing for her presence. After school in the evenings, I would wait for the magical sound of her footsteps coming home, still worried that she would vanish like my father. On Mother's Day each year I lavished her with presents, breakfast in bed, sentimental cards which invariably made her cry. One gift was a small china ornament decorated with red roses, displaying the verse:

Mother, I have a sweetheart,
And I would have no other.
She's more than all the world to me,
Because her name is Mother.

At the funeral, I had it placed on her coffin. It's now also on my piano.

Our love had an uncontaminated purity, enveloping us like a hundred warm blankets. When anyone asked me if I wanted to get married, I would grow cold, denying any such ambition. Not only did it carry the risk of another loss, it also signified a separation from the person to whom I had in essence felt 'married'. When James did in fact propose, that sense of dread returned, even though I was in love. I accepted, only with the reassurance that Mum was happy in my choice of partner. After Auntie Gwen died, I recognised that it was the first time in my entire life that I had my mother all to myself, and I looked forward to a period of renewal when we would rediscover that early untainted love, mend our differences. There are good memories of times she spent with me and James: we rented a lovely little bungalow in the heart of the New Forest for example, to celebrate together what was to be her last Christmas. She was also in York with us for James' 50th birthday party where she seemed to be in her element.

It has proved as hard therefore, if not harder, to write about the *'spikes in my skull'*, as the events in the preceding narrative. The comparative simplicity of the pain that came with the initial stages of grief almost felt a kind of gift: the price paid for love. I have questioned how much of a 'confessional' is appropriate here, asking myself (many times) what my mother would feel, reading the following pages. There is no way I would want to follow Prince Harry's somewhat vindictive example, but on the other hand, it would be dishonest to idealise our relationship. And I am sure she felt the same about me. Maybe it takes a lifetime to understand the interactions between ourselves and those closest to us. And to accept that none of us is perfect.

Initially I wrote in great detail about psychologically challenging experiences additional to the ones described here. Choosing afterwards to erase these was in itself healing, as though I were burying a rusty hatchet. In re-examining some other incidents I have reached a more profound understanding of Mum's own struggles with depression, frustration and disappointment. There was a need in me to forgive as well; bitterness was making me sour. I knew I had to move on to another, hopefully final, stage.

Going through Mum's papers after she died, I had found two old notebooks with a caption on the front reading:

'This is my life.'

The lengthy account had clearly been written at a time of deep despair. She wanted to remind me of the problems she had faced, (of which I had always been all too aware). At the same time she was at pains to thank me for being her 'friend'; for loving her as I did. I tried to assimilate these messages, in turn feeling rage at feeling 'dumped' again with her misery, then when I had calmed down later, pity and sadness. Maybe it was useful to hold on to these contradictions. More recently I have found myself questioning my own expectations of her, of motherhood in general. And let's face it, I have never been brave enough to take on the weighty task myself.

There was also a short note addressed to *'My beloved daughter',* which she must have written a couple of years after moving to Malvern Court. She described how she had been feeling very ill for a long time and in a great deal of pain, that life was no longer worth living. I was told not to grieve for her too much, that she was reassured that I had a wonderful husband to look after me. One last favour she asked of me was to ensure that Auntie Gwen had enough money to continue living at the complex as long as she needed. I was thanked for all the love we had shared and how this had sustained her.

When I had first read this note, not long after she died, I must have been in some sort of denial, for when I read it again only a few weeks ago whilst completing this memoir, I suspected that she had been contemplating suicide. What would that have done to me? Or to her own sister? My cousins? Her friends? The memory of a similar 'confession' she had made when I was quite young, returned. She had told me that one day not long after my father had died, she was waiting for an underground train to arrive and for a few moments had been tempted to throw herself on the line...

So my mother was indeed scarred by a number of experiences, not just early widowhood: her frustrations in relation to thwarted ambition; her feelings of having been 'used' by the family; her struggles financially; in old age coping with ill-health. Not long before she died she made a remark which indicated that she felt she had 'done nothing' with her life. Sad as this made me, it felt pointless to contradict her. But why on earth didn't I? On another occasion when I disclosed that I was seeing a therapist, she angrily retorted:

*'It's **me** who should be seeing a therapist, not you!'*

~

Perhaps the roots of this 'charged' relationship lay far back in time: something certainly changed when I reached puberty. I was becoming a sexual being when Mum was comparatively young and still sensing that empty space in her bed. She never re-married, in fact it seemed as though my Dad had been the only man for her. She still dreamt of him in old age.

Lately I read Sally Rooney's *'Beautiful World, Where Are You?'* How amazing that this young woman can write about 'it' so openly, especially as presumably her own parents are still alive. Wow. Although I can't possibly speak for everyone in my generation, the question of sex and sexuality was a taboo subject in our house. It was as though it had no place in our family.

Another scene. Mum and I are in the doctor's surgery as I am having what must have been hormonal symptoms. My mother was asked if I *'had been told yet'*. Mum's mumbled negative reply filled me with confusion. On the way back home she was unusually quiet and my imagination silently ran riot. Was I adopted? My aunt's illegitimate child? Or was I dying?

The next thing I knew was that responsibility for my sex education was passed to Auntie Gwen. Nothing was said, instead she gave me a book called *'Telling the Teenagers'*, whose sombre black and white cover of a group of miserable-looking youths, I still recall. Like many of my friends growing up in the 60s, this lack of healthy discussion (maybe I'm being idealistic), led to wild experimentation in my twenties, and to this day I thank God I didn't get pregnant. 'Going on the pill' was a guilt-inducing exercise. In the Family Planning Clinic in Cardiff, two nurses sat grimly behind a desk. I had no boyfriend at the time, but thought I should get some medication 'just in case'. And anyway, at that time it was fashionable.

'Does your mother know you're here?' one of them asked.

'Don't be daft' I thought. I gave a polite reply which didn't seem to prevent them from dishing out a few packets.

Sex continued as an unspoken subject between Mum and me. When I started dating, every boyfriend had to pass some kind of inspection. I fell desperately in love in my early twenties:

My Heathcliff

There was a bracelet and a seashell gathered in a storm,
worn to white polish through handling; dark curls on my lap;
that tender line of young skin. I felt his hurt like a cyst
ready to burst. There were no moors, but we roamed
the desolate valleys, deserted mines, tracing abandoned iron.

His name enough to make you swoon. We'd been schoolmates,
Encased in hatred, chips on shoulders, then met
across a crowded room. Gently inclined,
he had one ear on chat. I watched his back,
straight as a die. As he turned, the raven eye
was not what I had bargained for: it split the very root of me.

When I felt brave I took him home on approval,
but she was wary, as mothers are,
called him a devil, grew purple over red.

'I tell you girl, he's a no-good boyo:
all talk and no action.'

But there were connections: only child, dead father,
sad mother. Both of us scarred, lost, afraid,
tied to the rocks: visible but un-delighted.

In marrying James I felt I could breathe at last. But then the air thickened again. For the first Christmas that we spent together as man and wife, Mum and Auntie Gwen came to stay in our flat. For three weeks. One of James' colleagues declared: *'the shortest marriage in history?'*

By this time, we had moved into a ground floor Edwardian maisonette with a long corridor dividing the rooms. The early morning had Mum knocking loudly on our bedroom door indicating it was *'time to get up!'*, a pattern that continued in other locations when we were all together. I couldn't believe the pressure, the sense of invasion. During those three weeks I wanted to explode, escaping periodically by taking regular walks around the streets, trying to keep calm. On another occasion we were staying in Porthcawl. One Sunday morning James had gone out for a walk. I was in the kitchen when my mother arrived home from church, literally bursting in with:

'It's about time you gave him a baby! Everyone's asking me about it in church! What do I tell them?!'

I said nothing, as far as I remember. So whose life was it anyway? Whose body? Mine, or hers?

They also came to stay with us a few months after we had moved to York, following relocation by the British Library where James worked. My mother immediately started talking about wanting to move to be near us, had in fact spotted a flat in the same street. Arguments between her and her sister on the subject, the latter refusing to consider such a move, continued on and off for a few years. Once again I felt pulled in all directions.

The same issue inevitably cropped up after Auntie's death. Mum was now living alone in Malvern Court where she had established a number of friendships and as described, where she was extremely well cared for. I impressed upon her that James and I would give her every support in whatever decision she were to make about her future, pointing out what a move to be near us in York might involve in practical terms. Despite this attempt at helping her with such a difficult decision, she often loudly declared in front of me and her friends:

'My daughter doesn't want me!'

Looking back now, my response was always rather feeble, symptomatic no doubt of my own ambivalence: I was still aware of the pressures involved in dividing myself in two as daughter and wife. There was at the same time a feeling that anything I said at these moments would be twisted, as though she was always simply looking for rejection.

Moving on to those last few months in 2003, it was also Mum's decision alone to have the colonoscopy, no doubt in desperation as her symptoms were seriously disrupting her life, particularly socially. When I tried to talk to her about the possibility that these might have been partly due to her emotional state (not in so many words), she became defensive, scolding me for 'trying to analyse' her. I was aware for example that she was still grieving for her sister, also stressed about practical problems during the previous winter which I had been trying in vain at a significant distance to sort out. Reflecting on psychological issues such as the interplay between mind and body was never part of the culture in my mother's generation, so for me to raise it at that time was probably ill-advised. She saw it as a criticism, a sign of weakness, and coming from a daughter must have been especially hard to swallow.

There was no doubt a gulf between us, on top of the fact that the generation gap was much wider in the 60's. Maybe 'education' also played a part, something particularly significant perhaps amongst 'baby boomers' who were given so many opportunities to better ourselves. Like many others, I was the first person in my family to go to university. My childless aunts paid for me to go to a private junior school offering a fantastic grounding. They also funded piano, violin, elocution and ballet lessons, and at home I had access to my father's erudite book collection. Reading English literature in university and later undertaking social work training then opened up whole new worlds.

My mother, on the other hand, left school without qualifications at the age of 15. She was of course an intelligent and gifted woman, had so many practical skills which I entirely lack, but no means of safely understanding psychological processes, of reflecting on complex feelings and behaviours, which after all is not easy anyway. I remember her telling me that the night my father had died he was reading a book that struck her as *'very deep'*. She on many occasions told me *'you think too much'*, that I was *'too serious'* and even that I frightened her, which I assume (and hope) was a reference to these traits. I think it was significant that she admitted she could have benefitted from therapy and wish she had had the opportunity.

~

I wrote this poem not long after Mum's death. James and I were walking along the beach at Bamburgh on a cold winter's morning. A violent North Sea storm a few days before had stranded a baby seal, torn from the rocks and its mother:

It was an icy day, a new year. We held thickly-gloved hands,
raced like children down dunes. Some sea-monster sucked waves,
tossed foam; at the shore line strands of seaweed formed green hair.

The wind blew furrows whilst the sideways castle,
profiled against blue, frowned on. We spotted a dark shape,
and curious, headed out. There at the margin,

all brown eyes, glistening flippers, like a huge black almond,
it squirmed on, disabled, towards a patch of sunlight.
A couple with cold faces spoke of a storm:

'They get washed over, separated, then, stranded, can't get back.'

The bottomless eyes hooked into mine. Still twisting left and right,
it stared at rocks as if to seek some hidden causeway,
and curved its face aside.

My tears dotted the shifting sand.

Now, all these years later, the 'hidden causeway' strikes me as symbolic of that gulf in understanding. I was always searching for it.

Unkind words, insensitive actions, misunderstandings. Love and fury. Pride and disappointment. Joy and despair. Pleasure and pain in another's happiness. The opposites go on. Mum's words, spoken as they no doubt were from a place of intolerable psychic pain, still haunt me.

Losing Mum in such a dreadful way was bad enough, and the enquiry process utterly drained me. But not having had the opportunity to resolve these 'issues' in our relationship became like a sore that wouldn't heal. At last I became aware that it was I who had been picking away, and that maybe the inner conflict was my way of holding us together, of keeping her 'alive'. After a particularly distressing dream, I was able to write:

Cold Tea and Dust

Just when I thought I'd exorcised the guilt,
you creep again into dreams, slither in
between the sheets.

This time:
an unkempt house,
a tank of half-dead fish,
empty chairs, cold tea, dust
on window sills.

With my tears
I could the fill the universe:
melt the moon, wash away
the stars, drown the sea,
cast all the boats adrift.

But I'm alive and you are dead;
the moon's still there,
as is the sea, the whales, the fish,
and, dare I say, today the sun is out.

~

Afterword

There is no doubt that some questions cannot be answered, both in relation to the interaction between us and the nature of Mum's death. I will never know, for example, if she would have survived even had her care been exemplary. Also how would I have felt had she died more peacefully? Would the grieving have been any less prolonged? As it is, the final image in my mind is of her frantic eyes, like those of a cornered animal struggling for survival, together with the sight of her sucking desperately on oxygen, a picture no doubt familiar to those losing loved ones to Covid. A quiet, pain-free death is surely what we all long for, both for ourselves and those we love.

Also how each family approaches death and dying is important. Growing up, no one ever talked to me about my feelings in not having a father; in my family there didn't seem to be a 'healthy' model to follow in the handling of loss. You either held on to grief for dear life, or showed no feelings whatsoever. There was little sense of sharing, and when there was, it felt more like a competition. On one occasion when Mum and I were alone together, I tried to broach the subject of my father. Her response was that I *'couldn't have had a relationship with him'* as there had been little opportunity to spend much time together.

Despite everything, I continue to miss my mother profoundly, especially now as I make the journey into old age to face my own departure, not to mention the dread of losing James. Writing continues to nourish and enlighten: just one of the many creative arts that can ease heartache, which is why they are so important to our overall well-being. And why we must support them at all cost.

It has been interesting to note the difficulties I have had in feeling satisfied with this final part of my book. Goodness' knows how many times I revised the last section, and my comments here. It's so hard to let go, but let go I must.

The respect for those who care for others will hopefully lead to organisational reform. Likewise an understanding of individuals and families who are propelled into launching enquiries, would be a bonus. As we move forward work needs to be done in supporting the bereaved and the health and social care workers still struggling with symptoms of post-traumatic stress. This last week in October, watching the coverage of the Covid enquiry has reassured me that my story too, albeit 20 years old, must be shared. It is clear that the 'system' with its *'monolithic'* structures, led inevitably to miscommunication and lack of appropriate crisis planning. Moreover those losing elderly relatives must feel insulted by the intimation that this sector of the population *'should accept their fate'*. Maybe that too was an underlying attitude towards my mother and my aunt: that they didn't really 'matter' any more. These painful, glaring issues urgently require resolution.

But by whom?

One of the many gifts my mother passed on to me was her love of the natural world. There was nothing she liked better than to feel the sea between her toes, to admire a beautiful tree, a splendid sunset or the song of a bird. At the approach of spring this year whilst I was pressing on with the arduous task of assembling so many different narratives, I took a break to start working on the garden. When digging up one small patch, this little fellow joined me, clearly in search of the worms I would inevitably unearth.

The common Robin, like the 'common blue' butterfly I had admired sufficiently to honour with a poem, is generally thought of as the nation's bird, symbolising a whole host of positive messages, including hope, renewal, good luck, happiness and joy in life. It occurred to me recently that I might have missed other messages coming from my little visitor. I remember the way 'he' looked at me without fear, patiently waiting for his grub. I felt a connection.

Now we are at Halloween, a time when supposedly the boundary between the real and the spiritual world is thinner than usual. According to mythology the robin was regarded as a protector from storms and symbolic as conveying messages from the Universe, the Divine or Great Spirit. This tiny creature in its persistent quest for food reminds us to keep searching for what we need, however elusive it seems: in my case, inner peace after emotional and psychological turmoil.

The hard work of building a nest in the darkness of winter (being a very early nesting bird), can be a symbol of the power of determination, a quality I have thankfully inherited from my mother. Its cheerfulness a reminder that happiness is a choice, that there comes a time when mourning must end; its flight encouraging me to embrace the freedom of life, now that my responsibilities towards all my relatives, apart from James of course, are at an end.

The robin will eat the shells of its hatched chicks for extra calcium, a reminder to nourish ourselves, and it will feed the chicks of other species. So we must be kind. Its intelligence and resourcefulness contain an echo of our own innate wisdom and creativity. Its bright red breast symbolic of love and passion, the lovely splash of colour telling us to embrace beauty wherever we can.

Robins are plentiful, unlike so many other species they have learned to adapt to ever-changing circumstances, which I guess we must all strive to do, however bleak everything often feels, especially now when another ghastly war is destroying countless lives, young and old. Who knows what 2024 will bring.

Last but not least, some believe that seeing a robin may be a sign that those who have died are with us in spirit. I so hope my little friend survives the winter and comes back next year.

A poem certainly beckons.

~

Susan Elliot
October 2023

References

Astley, N. (ed) 2003 *'Staying Alive – real poems for unreal times'* Bloodaxe Books Ltd.

Bennett, Dr. A and Royle, Prof. N. 2009 *An Introduction to Literature Criticism and Theory* Pearson Education Ltd.

Bettleheim, B. 1991 *The Uses of Enchantment: The Meaning and Importance of Fairy Tales* Vintage Books

Freud, S. 1917 *Mourning and Melancholia* The Standard Edition of the Complete Psychological Works of Sigmund Freud, Volume X1V (1914 -16): On the History of the Psycho-analytic Movement, Papers on Metapsychology and Other Works, 237 – 258.

Hamilton, J.W. 1969 *Object Loss, Dreaming and Creativity – The Poetry of John Keats* in The Psychoanalytical Study of the Child 244 pages 488 - 531

Heaney, S. 1995 *The Redress of Poetry - Oxford Lectures* Faber and Faber Ltd.

Hollander, N. C. 1998 *Exile: Paradoxes of Loss and Creativity* British Journal of Psychotherapy 15(2)

Holmes, J. 1993 *John Bowlby and Attachment Theory* Routledge

Hunt, C. and Sampson, F. 2006 *Writing - self and reflexivity* Palgrave Macmillan

Kellaway, Kate *Into the Woods* /The Observer, Sunday 19 June 2005 rint" http://www.guardian.co.uk/books/2005/jun/19/poetry.features/print

Nabokov, V. (1982) 'The Art of Literature and Commonsense' in Bowers, F. (ed), Lectures on Literature. A Harvest Book

Parkes, C. M. 1975 *' Bereavement; Studies of Grief in Adult Life'* Penguin Books Ltd.

Secunda, V. in Exley, H. 1995 *The love between mothers and daughters - When you and your mother can't be friends* a Helen Exley giftbook Exley Publications Ltd.

Seighart, W. 2012 Preface to *The Forward Book of Poetry 2012* Forward Ltd.